The
Over-30
6-Week
All-Natural
Health
and Beauty
Plan

PHOTOGRAPHS BY GIDEON LEWIN
FOREWORD BY GRACE JORGENSEN, M.D.

CLARKSON N. POTTER, INC./PUBLISHERS   NEW YORK
DISTRIBUTED BY CROWN PUBLISHERS, INC.

The Over-30 6-Week All-Natural Health and Beauty Plan

BY ELIZABETH MARTIN

Inquiries should be addressed to Clarkson N. Potter, Inc.,
One Park Avenue, New York, New York 10016

Printed in the United States of America

Published simultaneously in Canada by General Publishing Company Limited

Library of Congress Cataloging in Publication Data

Martin, Elizabeth, 1942–
    The over-30, 6-week, all-natural health and
beauty plan.

    1. Middle aged women—Health and hygiene.
2. Beauty, Personal.   I. Title.   II. Title: The over-
thirty, six-week, all-natural health and beauty plan.
RA778.M362   1982   613'.04244   81-17719
ISBN: 0-517-544393   AACR2

Designed by Betty Binns Graphics

10 9 8 7 6 5 4 3 2 1

FIRST EDITION

To my
former and
future
students

Acknowledgments

Without the help and support of the following people, this book would not have been possible. I wish to acknowledge and thank each and every one of them for their valuable contributions.

My husband, Dick Campana, and daughter, Eve, for their love and patience.

My mother, Helen E. Saunders, and my mother-in-law, Jennie Campana, for the many unselfish hours of child care.

My editor, Carolyn Hart, for her invaluable assistance in the publication of this book.

My friend, Anne M. Hubbard, Ph.D., whose initial encouragement precipitated the writing of this book.

My sister-in-law, Ann Fusco, and my assistant, Lynn Kelleher, for their time and effort spent typing the manuscript.

My friend and physician, Grace Jorgensen Westney, M.D., for all her assistance.

Alan Epstein, M.D., senior research associate at the Orentreich Foundation, who gave me much valuable information about skin care for this book.

My photographer, Gideon Lewin.

My hairstylist, Heather Lloyd-MacDonald.

My makeup artist, Terry Shank.

Contents

Foreword

FIFTY years ago my family founded Bellevue Maternity Hospital, dedicated to the special health needs of women in our community that at the time were not being met by other health-care institutions. Today, I am pleased to see more women becoming aware that their health needs *are* special and more health professionals trying to address their concerns in a positive and meaningful way. Elizabeth Martin's health and beauty program works, in my opinion, because she is sensitive to women's special problems. As a physician, I know that there are certain basic physiological differences between men and women; Elizabeth respects those differences while encouraging women to become stronger, healthier, more beautiful, and therefore more secure in themselves.

At Bellevue we have delivered over 60,000 babies, and I am daily reminded that each of us at birth is given the priceless gifts of natural beauty and health. The responsibility for the preservation and maintenance of these gifts is up to the individual, however. A great deal of illness and unattractiveness can be prevented simply by learning to know one's body and taking care of it, and by slowing down and enjoying life to the fullest.

I have known Elizabeth for ten years and have personally seen her inspire many women to make positive changes in their lives. I have seen her program work when medical efforts were less successful. I know of no other book that combines health and beauty concerns in such an integrated way, and I think this is one of the reasons the plan is so effective. She wisely puts nutrition first (without which good health is impossible) and then gradually adds exercise, skin care, posture, stress control, and so on, so that by the end of her course, improvement is noted in the *whole* person.

There is much that women of all ages can learn from this valuable book. With it, they will be able to help themselves lead happier, healthier lives and achieve their maximum potential as women.

Grace Jorgensen, M.D.
Medical Director, Bellevue Hospital,
Schnectady, New York
December 1981

Introduction

E VEN though you are over thirty, you can look more beautiful, feel more energetic, and like yourself better than you ever thought possible—all within the next few weeks! All you need is the desire to look and feel your best and the willingness to work at it; I'll provide the method. Now, before you put this book aside thinking, "Another cockeyed optimist," let me explain how I know that this statement is a reality, not just a daydream.

Seventeen years ago, at the age of twenty-two, I was an aspiring model. As a teenager I had been plump and self-conscious, with a lot of weight unevenly distributed below the waist. When I went for an initial interview at a model agency, the director looked at me skeptically and said, "Unless you lose twenty pounds and get rid of those heavy legs, you'll never be a model." At that point, my desire to look like the pretty women in the magazines was strong, and I determined to do something quickly to reshape my body. Three months later I went back to the model agency, and the director couldn't believe the changes I had made. By strict dieting and very high repetition exercises (some of which are in my program today) I had lost twenty-five pounds and reshaped my body from 38½-26-40 to 37-23-34½. I was immediately asked to become a junior member of the physical culture staff of the agency's school. I worked as both a model and a teacher, eventually becoming assistant director and then acting director of the modeling school.

At the end of 1970 another model and I decided to open our own school. I also began to teach physical culture on television, and met some very impressive health care professionals through my affiliation with the TV station. However, I was still not aware of the relationship between health and beauty. I thought of eating strictly in terms of calories, and paid little attention to nutrition. Along with other models, I often had skin and hair trouble, broken fingernails, and many other health-related problems, which we managed to camouflage with carefully applied makeup, hairpieces, and other tricks of the trade. Not so easy to camouflage was a frequent lack of energy, or the highs and lows of mood swings caused by stringent dieting and too little relaxation.

In early 1971 a crisis in my life changed its course forever. One Saturday evening my husband and I were invited to dinner at a friend's home and enjoyed a lot of rich food, sauces, sweets, and wine. When I woke up Sunday morning, I weighed ten pounds more than the day before! Terribly frightened, I called a doctor, and she asked to see me immediately, explaining that either I had experienced kidney failure or I was pregnant and had developed toxemia. Tests confirmed my pregnancy. Dr. Jorgensen explained that my sudden weight gain was due to excessive fluid retention caused in part by pregnancy and also by poor diet. She advised me that if I didn't tend to my diet, serious consequences could result. My years of crash-dieting to remain model-thin had finally caught up with me. Sensing my concern, Dr. Jorgensen asked me kindly, "How would you like to look and feel better than you ever have? You can, if you learn to eat right. There's no reason to gain a lot of weight during your pregnancy, or to get stretch marks and varicosities. You can continue to work right up to the last month, and there's no reason why you can't teach exercises on your TV program, either." I decided then and there to follow the program of nutrition outlined by Dr. Jorgensen. She herself was a living example of the benefits of healthy eating—she was a radiant woman of unbelievable energy.

Two weeks after I began my new dietary program, changes began to occur—my skin improved dramatically, my fingernails grew stronger, the whites of my eyes became clearer and shinier, my hair grew faster and shinier, I lost all of my bloat, and best of all, my energy level soared. In three months I was happier and healthier than I had ever dreamed possible. I worked until a week before I gave birth, and wore a leotard on my TV show until the beginning of the ninth month. And during my pregnancy, whenever I had a chance, I studied nutrition. Dr. Carleton Fredericks, Linda Clark, Gayelord Hauser, and Dr. Wilfrid Schute became my paperback friends. Cautiously at first, I began to teach my student models what I had learned—and what wonderful results we had! They too saw improvements in the condition of their skin, hair, nails, eyes, and teeth, and experienced the energy that occurs when the body is in an optimum state of health.

The years since then have been busy ones, spent in teaching, research, working with the media, and exploring diverse areas of health and beauty. I take an active interest in swimming, skiing, traveling, yoga, weight-training, and ballet. As a wife and mother, I experience many joys, but also many responsibilities. I am now thirty-nine years old; my life is varied, interesting, and challenging, but I still find time to care for myself. I learned a long time ago that health and a feeling of pride in appearance are basic to enjoying life in general. Through my work I have met many truly beautiful women over thirty, forty, fifty, and beyond who attract attention, admiration, and love from all who meet them. These women serve as a powerful inspiration to me, reminding me that as we get older it is natural to get better, and that the necessary time allotted to health and beauty produces a payoff that extends into every facet of life.

Since I began my teaching career, I have wondered why individualized health and beauty programs are not available to all women, not just to very wealthy women, models, and actresses. In 1974, with an experimental group of six students of various ages and backgrounds, I began a six-week program of health and beauty. The first week we worked on diet, the second on Body Sculpting (our exercise program), the third week on skin care, the fourth week on posture, the fifth week on relaxation, and at the sixth meeting on a lifetime maintenance program. Within just six weeks, unbelievable changes occurred. My phone began to ring as friends of the original group asked to participate in the program. Within eight months, two hundred students had completed the program, which was then held in my home. I did not advertise at all—the newfound beauty and health of my students attracted others to the program.

Since then, I have taught women of all ages how to reach their peak of health and beauty. The myth that physical well-being and radiant beauty belong only to the very young is nonsense. Thank heavens the media in this country is finally beginning to realize this. Magazines like *Vogue* and *Harper's Bazaar* are featuring fashions and makeup techniques for the over-thirty woman, and television and motion pictures are utilizing the talents of more mature actresses and casting them in glamorous roles. Recently a poll was taken to determine the "ten most beautiful women," as perceived by the French public—seven of the ten women chosen were over forty! Women such as Jane Fonda, Ali MacGraw, Lena Horne, Ann Miller, Sophia Loren, and Gloria Swanson—to name just a few—are proof positive that over thirty is definitely not over the hill. They are vital, creative, involved, and gorgeous! The body of *any* age responds quickly and positively to loving care—and, unfortunately, just as quickly to disinterest and abuse. Now that you are over thirty, no doubt you have many new interests, duties, and responsibilities, in terms of both family and career. I understand, because so do I, and so do my students. But I still maintain that you can find the time to look and feel your best, and I strongly believe that you owe it to yourself.

Results with this program come quickly; in one to two weeks you will begin to see changes. You *can* have the kind of figure you always wanted. There's no need to suffer with cellulite any longer—the program will help you get rid of that, too. Your skin will become prettier and your eyes brighter, your nails and hair will grow longer and stronger, and you will have more energy. You will learn the secrets of posture that have created an aura of beauty for models and dancers from time immemorial, and you will experience the serenity that comes with release from stress.

Will this program be expensive? No—you will spend your money more wisely, concerned with quality instead of quantity.

Will this program be terribly time-consuming? No. In the beginning you will probably have to spend 45 minutes a day on the exercise program, but after your best measurements are achieved, 20 minutes a day will be enough. You will save time on grocery and shopping trips because you will know beforehand exactly what you want. Meal planning will become easier. Remember, my students are busy women like you—businesswomen, homemakers, teachers, doctors, and writers. Think of the first few weeks as a learning process, and plan to spend a little time on a regimen that will reap a lifetime of rewards.

Does this program involve any special equipment? No, and it can be practiced anywhere—at home, on vacation, or on a business trip.

Will this program be enjoyable? Yes—it is designed for pleasure, not for deprivation. I really believe that beauty and health are two of the most positive aspects of life, and that they can be attained easily and joyfully. Of course, in order to achieve any desired result some discipline must always be employed, but there is no need to be miserable in order to look and feel good. I am sure that soon you will look forward each day to your program.

Although this book is intended primarily for women over thirty, anyone, including men and children, can benefit from the program. You may want to incorporate it into your family life, as I and many of my students have done.

Join me in dispelling the myth of "downhill after thirty." Let's prove that you're more beautiful and vital than ever!

Week One

Eating for Beauty and Health

FROM experience—my own and my students'—I am convinced that diet, at any age but especially after thirty, is the cornerstone of health and beauty. Just as an expensive sports car needs high-octane fuel and regular maintenance to run smoothly and keep its appearance, so does the intricate and finely tuned human body need high-quality food and careful attention to operate at peak performance and retain (or regain) its sleek lines. Surely you are more important than your car and deserve at least comparable care and attention. You know what happens when you neglect your automobile: Paint peels and fades; the body rusts; the engine overheats, sputters, stalls, and eventually refuses to run at all. And yet, how often we take our bodies for granted, sometimes neglecting their most basic needs. No wonder they respond with poor skin, cellulite, falling hair, split nails, bruises, wrinkles, sags, bags, overweight or underweight. Fortunately, the human body is so resilient that we can reclaim our birthright of health and beauty relatively quickly with attention to diet, physical fitness, posture, skin, and stress control. Many of the conditions mentioned above will miraculously disappear once you begin to love yourself a little.

You are a beautiful person, and right this minute you are going to begin to feed your marvelous body only with what will nourish and beautify it. You will no longer insult yourself with debilitated foods of poor quality that ultimately produce unhealthiness and unhappiness.

Protein for Beauty and Health

An important element of your diet is an adequate intake of high-quality, or complete, protein. Protein is needed for good hair, skin, and nails; it builds and repairs body tissues, builds good blood, and balances body processes.

Most of us consume adequate amounts of protein, but we often obtain it from poor (incomplete) sources, or consume heavy proteins at night, when the body processes are slowing down. Many beauty experts believe that, for optimum physical attractiveness, 1 gram of high-quality protein should be consumed per day for every 2 pounds of body weight. Thus, if your ideal weight is 120 pounds, 60 grams of protein per day will keep you looking and feeling your best.

Here are some easily obtained high-quality proteins:

Chicken	3 ounces	= 14 grams protein
Turkey	3 ounces	= 18 grams protein
Calves' liver	3 ounces	= 18 grams protein
Veal	4 ounces	= 15 grams protein
Tuna	3 ounces	= 25 grams protein
Salmon	3 ounces	= 17 grams protein
Haddock	3 ounces	= 16 grams protein
Swordfish	3 ounces	= 24 grams protein
Skim milk	1 cup	= 9 grams protein
Hard cheese	1 ounce	= 7 grams protein
Cottage cheese	½ cup	= 20 grams protein
Low-fat plain yogurt	1 cup	= 8 grams protein
Egg	1	= 6 grams protein
Brewer's yeast	1 tablespoon	= 8 grams protein

This list will help you get started. Very detailed protein gram counters listing many foods can be purchased in any stationery store for about a dollar.

The sources I've listed are complete proteins: They contain all the amino acids the body needs. Fruits and vegetables, grains, and legumes generally contain incomplete proteins, which can be fully utilized by the body when combined with complementary incomplete proteins. For example, combining beans and a wheat product yields a complete protein. Very dark green vegetables contain a complete protein comparable to high-quality milk protein.

If you want to eliminate animal protein from your diet entirely, you have my blessing. I know many people who suffered from severe allergies, arthritis, and skin problems for years until they adopted a meatless diet. If you decide that vegetarianism is definitely for you, make sure to learn to balance your proteins. Three cookbooks that I can recommend with confidence are Frances Moore Lappé's *Diet for a Small Planet,* Ellen Ewald's *Recipes for a Small Planet,* and Joy Gross's *30-Day Way to a Born-Again Body.*

CAN YOU CONSUME TOO MUCH PROTEIN?

The answer is definitely yes. While it is important to consume an optimum amount of protein for your body weight, too much protein definitely can be harmful. Dr. Alan Immerman, who is the director of research for the American Natural Hygiene Society and consultant to the Pawling Health Manor at Hyde Park, New York, told me that some of the dangers of excess protein intake include acceleration of the aging process, build-up of fats in the arteries (which can eventually cause heart attacks and stroke), loss of essential calcium, and intestinal toxemia. Be aware that many low-carbohydrate, "quick-weight-loss" diets, which sanction the consumption of large amounts of protein, can do far more harm than good. Adjust your intake to your ideal body weight and do not exceed it.

There are two sources of complete protein that I want you to eliminate from your diet completely: beef and pork. In my experience, both are detrimental to beauty and health. They are very high in calories, very high in animal fat, and full of preservatives in most cases (nitrates and nitrites in pork, DES in beef, all possibly carcinogenic). In addition, most pork products are loaded with salt, which causes fluid retention in the body tissues. One of the beauty benefits of eliminating beef and pork is a clearer complexion—without exception my students have noticed a refining of the pores and a more translucent appearance of the facial skin. After a month or so of abstinence they find that they no longer enjoy the taste of beef or pork; when they eat these meats occasionally, they feel uncomfortable, bloated, and sluggish after the meal. I myself was once a pound-a-day steak eater, but now I have no desire even to taste beef—I just don't like the "heavy" feeling that results, and I don't like the way I look the next day, either. One final note: If you have any problems with cellulite (those lumpy deposits of fat, water, and toxins that can stubbornly accumulate under a woman's skin), avoid muscle meats at all costs. They definitely aggravate the condition.

Replace the heavy, bloating meats with wonderful varieties of chicken, turkey, veal, seafood, cheese, and eggs. You will cut your calorie count way down. For the most part, also avoid such meats as lamb and duck, because they tend to be fatty. However, they generally do not contain preservatives, or as many calories as beef or pork, so if you really love them, include them in your diet on special occasions only.

IS BREAKFAST IMPORTANT? YOU BET IT IS!

It is absolutely necessary, for optimum energy, to eat a nutritious breakfast that contains an adequate amount of protein. What is an adequate amount? At least one-fourth of your optimum protein level. We know that protein helps keep the blood sugar level of the body stable longer than foods containing sugar, which raises the blood sugar only to have it drop quickly. What does a stable high blood sugar level mean? It means feeling energetic, optimistic, and productive—

21

comfortably full. "I don't have time to eat breakfast" is an oft-heard complaint from my students, so my diet includes some nutritious, delicious "instant" meals that will satisfy even the most discriminating appetite on the most harried schedule.

Water—the Wonder Drink

Another important staple of my Over-30 Diet is pure, uncarbonated spring water. Most people today don't like water, and with good reason. Tap water is chlorinated and fluoridated, resulting in a generally dreadful taste. Worse, the additives in tap water can be detrimental to your health—recent research links chlorine to cancer. Pure spring water is delicious, refreshing, and filling. The best source is tested well or spring water. Try to find a natural spring in your area (many U.S. cities have spring sites) and collect your drinking water from it. If none is available, spring or still mineral water can be purchased from your supermarket. Under no circumstances should you purchase carbonated waters; they are bloating and usually contain large amounts of sodium.

I'll bet you're thinking, "But if I drink all that water, I'll hold fluid, won't I?" The answer is emphatically no. You will activate your kidneys to flush impurities from your system, which will result in a much clearer, translucent complexion and the loss of that old bugaboo, cellulite. Spring water, sipped between meals, is a delicious alternative to coffee and diet soda, two cellulite makers and health robbers that we certainly can do without. In addition, water is the best possible moisturizer for skin, and the intake of adequate amounts of pure water can plump up the cells from within and actually make the skin appear younger. Eight glasses of spring water per day are mandatory on your diet.

From now on, don't eat and drink at the same time. This is a conditioned habit. Try to take fluids one half hour before a meal, and wait an hour afterward. (An exception to this rule is the instant meal, which is a liquid anyway.) When I was a young model, my teacher told me that eating and drinking at the same time would result in a bloated abdomen. (Have you ever felt the need to loosen your belt and unzip your jeans after eating?) Later, I learned that there is another, even more important reason: Liquids taken with solids dilute the digestive enzymes that assimilate nutrients, so food is not absorbed properly. For the first few days on this plan you will have to monitor yourself at mealtime, but when you notice how nice and flat your tummy remains after dinner, you will want to continue this healthy habit permanently.

Eliminate the Negative

To look and feel your very best, it will be necessary to break some old, negative, self-defeating food patterns. I promise you, this will not be difficult, and after only two weeks (in many cases immediately) you will wonder what you ever enjoyed about the poor-quality food you have banished forever from your life.

PRESERVATIVES

First and foremost, begin to read labels. It is not enough for a food to be labeled "natural"; very often labels are misleading—deliberately, I'm afraid. A new FTC proposal, which will hopefully become law this year, would require that in order to be advertised as "natural" products may not contain synthetic or artificial ingredients and may not be more than minimally processed. This law should result in tighter controls on manufacturers who exploit the word "natural," but as of this writing, it's consumer beware.

23

Remember that preservatives are one of the most common causes of cellulite, allergies, and bloat. In addition, many preservatives formerly regarded as safe have been proven carcinogenic, and statistics warn us that the cancer rate will continue to rise because of the many ingested and external pollutants in our lives. We must take responsibility for our own health and beauty! It is worth a few minutes of reading labels until choosing safe brands becomes second nature to you. An excellent paperback, *The Supermarket Guide to Additive Free Foods*, may be purchased in any bookstore, and many community health organizations publish pamphlets that list additive-free foods and stores that sell them.

OVER-THE-COUNTER DRUGS

Next, eliminate as much as possible over-the-counter drug preparations. Often these concoctions cause more problems than they "cure," and almost weekly now comes a report that one or another of them is being taken off the market because of undesirable side effects. Don't be a guinea pig! As you become more healthy and relaxed on this program, you will have far fewer headaches, colds, bouts of insomnia, and indigestion that send you running to the medicine chest. If you suffer from poor elimination (a real beauty and health problem), unprocessed miller's bran added to your breakfast drink, or to some fresh applesauce, will provide bulk for your intestinal tract and help regulate your system. The raw foods on the diet should help, too. Determine the amount of bran that is right for you. Some people do well with a teaspoon a day, while others (especially those under stress) may need as much as a half cup or more.

SUGAR

It is becoming common knowledge that sugar is a highly detrimental and addictive substance that can wreak havoc with our bodies. Scores of researchers, including Carleton Fredericks, Richard Passwater, Emanual Chereskin, and Alan Cott, have warned that sugar is one of the most insidious enemies of well-being. Excess weight, depression, cravings, nervousness, and even underweight are all directly attributable to the sugar habit. Sugar contains "empty calories" and creates a host of problems.

Why do we crave sugar? Because when we consume it, it causes the blood sugar level to skyrocket suddenly, triggering the pancreas to produce insulin at an accelerated rate. As a result of this overactivity, the blood sugar then drops sharply, leaving us weak, depressed, and hungry, and we crave sugar to make the blood sugar level rise all over again. It's a vicious cycle.

A serious condition called hypoglycemia can be caused by the excessive consumption of sugar. If you are very depressed or irritable or have blackouts or tremors when you must go without sugar for even a little while, I strongly suggest that you contact a nutritionally oriented physician and take a six-hour glucose tolerance test to determine your blood sugar level. Since hypoglycemia can lead to diabetes, and also affect your emotional state, it is well worth it to nip this condition in the bud.

Many women crave sugar a week before the menses. Researchers now believe that the rise in estrogen precipitates a temporary hypoglycemic condition. Experts advise that sugar cravings can be cut way down by the ingestion of small amounts of protein foods every two to three hours, which raises and stabilizes the blood sugar level.

The best way to eliminate sugar is to banish it altogether right now. Cutting down won't do. "How can I do it when I love sugar?" I can hear some of you moan. When you begin to eat for health and beauty, and include foods that will stabilize your blood sugar level and supplements that will make you more serene, you will no longer need the "quick fix" that sugar

25

provides. After two weeks of avoiding sugar completely, you will lose your taste for it, and your resultant health and beauty will motivate you to avoid it forever.

If you are a confirmed sugar addict (I once was, so I know how it feels), you may wish to become familiar with a wonder nutrient available in health food stores that can help you get over the sugar habit. It's an amino acid called L-glutamine. Glutamic acid and glucose (blood sugar) share a special function—they are both fuel for the brain and provide high energy. Richard Passwater, Ph.D., Roger Williams, Ph.D., and nutritionist H. L. Newbold, M.D., are some of the pioneers in L-glutamine research. As an experimental nutritional approach, the researchers suggest 600–1000 mg per day the first week, 1200–1500 mg per day the second week, and 2 gm per day the third week and thereafter, if necessary, to control the sugar craving. Peter Andrus, M.D., who is a highly respected megavitamin therapist in the upstate New York area, assured me that this dosage is perfectly safe. Although L-glutamine is not an essential part of my Over-30 program, I do recommend it to my students who have trouble giving up sugar, and you may wish to try it yourself.

In addition to controlling the sweet tooth, L-glutamine is experimentally being used in the treatment of alcoholism. Alcohol is converted quickly to sugar in the bloodstream, and many authorities believe that alcoholism is often a manifestation of hypoglycemia. (The main symptom of hypoglycemia is an excessive craving for sugar.)

"Can't I ever enjoy baked goods again? What about holidays?" you ask. Of course you may enjoy goodies in moderation, if weight is not a problem for you, but in place of the debilitating, overprocessed, chemically laden, sugary commercial products and mixes, you can easily—and much more deliciously—substitute products baked with whole-grain flours, raw honey, fresh fruit, and nuts. You'll never miss sugar again.

HARD LIQUOR

I am not against a light, dry, naturally fermented wine taken in moderation, unless you suffer from cellulite (in which case you must limit yourself to two 3½-ounce glasses per week) or are overweight (in which case I recommend no alcohol until your correct weight has been achieved—alcohol is an appetite stimulant). I am totally against all forms of hard liquor, which can accelerate the aging process, and certainly contributes to the cellulite problem. In many people, alcohol ingestion can burst the tiny blood vessels close to the skin, causing a blotchy and uneven complexion. Alcohol can also produce acne rosacea, an adult form of acne that results in facial disfiguration.

A glass or two of dry wine taken before dinner on the weekend can relax you and heighten the enjoyment of your meal, and of your dinner companions, but more than that should be avoided. (A 3½-ounce glass of dry white wine is 74 calories; the same amount of dry red wine is 81 calories.) Anyway, you won't need alcohol to relax because you'll be feeling so good from this program!

SALT

The overuse of salt is one of the main causes of female figure problems. Women have an extra layer of fat that men don't have, which may be why we are more prone to overweight and why it is more difficult for us to lose weight. Also, we experience almost constant hormonal fluctuations, which in themselves lead to a tendency to fluid retention. Add too much sodium chloride (salt) to this already problematic situation, and what do we have? Bloated waistlines, tummies, knees, thighs, ankles, and hands, not to mention the blossoming of cellulite, an accumulation of toxic wastes. Salt occurs naturally in many of the foods we eat. It is not necessary for us to add one iota of table salt to obtain adequate amounts of this substance.

In this country, we have been raised with the salt shaker on the table. No wonder we see cellulite blooming all about us! Not to mention heart and blood pressure problems. Like sugar, salt is addictive. I've often wondered about the overuse of salt in fast and processed foods. If an unethical manufacturer can hook someone on an addictive substance, the customer will keep coming back to buy, won't she? Not only that, but salt, because of its flavor-enhancing properties, can mask poor-quality foods. Within two weeks of eliminating salt entirely, you'll never miss it, I promise you. As a matter of fact, you soon won't be able to abide salty foods at all. After only a week of eliminating salt, when you look in the mirror, or take your measurements, you'll swear off it forever!

Beware of hidden sources of sodium, like diet soda or any carbonated beverage (including so-called "natural" carbonated water). Replace these bloating, chemical drinks with delicious pure spring water. Avoid canned foods (unless the label states that no sugar or salt has been added), luncheon meats, corned beef, "instant" foods (salad dressings, dips, powdered cream substitutes, sauces and gravies, dessert toppings), and white pasta. Be careful, too, with foods made with baking soda or baking powder, because these substances contain sodium chloride.

Remember, our convenience lifestyle is mainly responsible for the cellulite that is so epidemic in our country. I promise that you won't have to spend a lot of time slaving over a hot stove in order to make meals delicious on this program. So, out with convenience foods!

In place of salt, first and foremost, determine never again to purchase foods of inferior quality. Since you are eliminating junk foods from your life (and the junk is really expensive), replace them with the best meat and produce you can find. Contact your local Jewish community center and locate a good kosher butcher (kosher meat contains no preservatives), or hunt down an organic farmer in your area. Most cities and towns have at least one superior fresh fruit and vegetable market. You won't be spending any more money for first-quality food than you did for junk (as a matter of fact, you'll probably spend less). With this fine-quality food, you won't need salt. But you can add various herbs and spices to enhance flavor and add interest. To get you started:

Freshly ground pepper (you should have a pepper mill)	enhances the flavor of meat, vegetables, salads, eggs, fish, stews, and soups
Dill	for salad dressings, dips, eggs, noodles, tomatoes, casseroles, fish
Allspice	for beets, carrots, spinach, soups, sauces
Basil	for salad dressings, tomato sauces
Cinnamon	for fruit dishes
Juniper berries	for soups and sauces
Marjoram	for veal and soups
Nutmeg	for chicken, peas, broccoli, cabbage, puddings, and some milk drinks
Rosemary	for eggs, meat, spinach, cauliflower, and broccoli
Turmeric	for eggs and fish
Tarragon	for cheese, celery, tomatoes, peas, green beans, salads, eggs, and poultry
Thyme	for veal and most vegetables

Three other ingredients that will add a bouquet to almost any dish (except fruits and dessert) are:

Fresh garlic	a natural blood purifier, as well as a tasty addition to many foods; add it to sauces, salads, fish, and meat
Minced onion	adds spice to meat, potatoes, casseroles, and vegetables
Chives	combine well with cheese, butter, yogurt, cottage cheese, soups, stews, sauces, salads, eggs, and fish

Finally, in the health food store or gourmet shop you will find two products that are convenient to use and delicious: Vegebase, a combination of herbs that enlivens any vegetable or meat dish, and Gayelord Hauser's Vegit, eighteen ingredients (and *no* salt) in a single bottle, which is wonderful sprinkled over steamed vegetables.

To learn more about good cooking without salt, I recommend reading *Craig Claiborne's Gourmet Diet Cookbook*.

CAFFEINE

I know that many of you depend on coffee, tea, or cola to get you through the day. In our stress-filled and rush-rush competitive society, we often turn to caffeine, desperate for energy. Unfortunately, caffeine is a deceptive drug, and an addictive one as well. Like sugar, it provides a quick lift, followed by a quick letdown. Not only that, but caffeine destroys Vitamin B, which we need for our nerves, increases sensitivity to the sun, and is responsible for anxiety, insomnia, hostility, and even, according to recent research, for breast cysts. Three of my students have reported the disappearance of breast congestion since they eliminated caffeinated beverages. Many of my students who suffered from dark under-eye circles noticed a rapid and progressive lightening of this area after giving up coffee. Every one of them reports a general increase in well-being, less tension, fewer mood swings, and better skin tone. Caffeine aggravates cellulite, too.

Cheryl Baker, thirty, came to me in the midst of preparations for her wedding. Naturally, she wanted to look and feel her best, but she was living with horrible headaches, her nerves were shot, and her work and personal life were suffering. Her doctor had been treating her with pain-killers for her migraine headaches and Valium for relief from tension. I learned that Cheryl drank large amounts of caffeinated beverages and had very poor eating habits, which include the consumption of fast foods. I asked her to eliminate the drugs she was taking, as well as caffeine, salt, and beef, and follow my nutritional program. In only two weeks, she was calmer, her headache pain greatly lessened. Eventually her headaches virtually disappeared. At present, when under a lot of pressure, she still sometimes gets a headache, but one aspirin tablet usually takes care of it. The circles under her eyes have disappeared, and she looks wonderful.

If you are a heavy caffeine user, as Cheryl was, for a day or two you may experience a headache or feeling of lethargy. Your system is detoxifying from this drug, and the discomfort is a sign that your body is eliminating the offender. Ride it out. The discomfort will be replaced by a new vitality, emotional stability, and healthy beauty that will be far more enticing to you than endless cups of coffee or tea. You will soon wonder why you ever punished your system with this unhealthy and unbeautiful drug.

There are some alternatives to coffee and tea. Pero, Bambu, and Caffix are three grain beverages that are widely used as coffee substitutes. I do not recommend decaffeinated coffee (with the exception of water-decaffeinated coffees now available in gourmet shops), because it contains chemicals that some researchers believe may be carcinogenic.

Herbal teas have become popular in recent years. One brand, Celestial Seasonings, is widely available in supermarkets as well as health food stores. Herbal teas have many uses—chamomile tea is wonderfully soothing in the evening and helps to promote restful sleep (it is also used in Europe to alleviate menstrual cramps and labor pains); alfalfa mint tea helps cleanse the system of toxins and is useful to cellulite sufferers; chilled red zinger tea, doctored with a little fresh lemon juice, a slice of orange, a dash of grape juice, and raw honey makes a delicious nonalcoholic alternative to red wine. One cautionary note: Although I personally have never come across anyone allergic to herbal teas, some pharmacists warn that when taken in excess, herbal teas can produce allergic reactions, especially in people predisposed to respiratory allergies.

If you prefer regular tea, decaffeinated versions are now on the market as well. Wagner's, for instance, has perfected delicious gourmet decaffeinated teas such as English Breakfast, Earl Grey, and Cinnamon and Spice.

Another satisfying hot drink is a cup of hot spring water with a squeeze of lemon. And, of course, you will be drinking lots of refreshing spring water as part of the program.

Colas and diet sodas of all types are not part of the diet, not only because of the caffeine content but because of the carbonation, which causes bloating in all the wrong places. Cut them out entirely, substitute your delicious alternatives for them, and within two weeks they'll just be a bad memory.

To recap briefly: Today you are going to banish forever from your life all added salt and sugar, carbonated beverages, caffeine, hard liquor, instant and overprocessed foods, chemical preservatives, white-flour products, beef, pork, and highly processed meats.

Vitamins

Over the years, I have become a strong believer in vitamins, but I recognize that the vitamin issue is a controversial one.

There are those who maintain that there is no need for supplementation when an optimum diet is eaten. That *is* true, I agree, for those who are able to lead perfect lives! However, there are several conditions today that make it virtually impossible for anyone to receive all the nutrients the body requires from food alone.

We know that the best foods are "live" foods—produce, for instance, that is picked straight from the garden, washed, and eaten immediately. Fresh foods lose vital nutrients very quickly, and storage, processing, and heating deplete their nutritional value even more. In addition, in times past the soil was given time to "rest" between crops, and consequently it was much more fertile and the foods grown upon it were more nutritious.

Our bodies were designed to be physically active. Ideally we should eat large quantities of fresh food and then burn the calories off with vigorous physical exercise, as our ancestors did. However, we live today in a convenience society, and if we consume the large numbers of calories required for optimum nutrition, we will become overweight.

Finally, that monster of modern-day life, stress, burns up water-soluble vitamins with incredible speed. Negative food substances like caffeine, alcohol, and sugar compound the stress while destroying stress-fighting vitamins; and in women, the hormonal cycle itself creates an additional physical stress. These are the indisputable facts of modern life. It only makes sense to ensure our health with judicial amounts of water soluble vitamins.

As a beauty professional, I can state unequivocally that the vitamins I recommend in this plan will do much to improve your appearance and help keep you youthful. As a matter of fact, I have never met another beauty professional who did not attest to the positive effect of vitamins in the maintenance and rejuvenation of both skin and hair. I noticed a dramatic improvement in both my appearance and my energy level as soon as I began a personal megavitamin program. When, experimentally, I stopped for a few days, negative results were apparent in both my energy level and my mood. I didn't wait for my appearance to be affected!

Over the years I have been fortunate in meeting many dedicated physicians in the field of vitamin therapy. My education began when I met Dr. Wilfrid Schute, of Vitamin E fame, in 1971. He was a guest on my television segment and, upon learning of my interest in nutrition, spent considerable time explaining his findings and studies to me. I was impressed with the results of his work and passed my knowledge on to my TV viewers, many of whom called to let me know of their positive experiences with vitamins. Since that time, through much research, education, and experience, both personal and professional, I have become convinced that megavitamin therapy will become one of the best preventive and curative treatments available to us in the field of medicine. If you want to explore megavitamin therapy more thoroughly, you can consult a nutritionally oriented medical doctor trained to evaluate your body's specific vitamin and mineral needs. For further reading, I recommend *Supernutrition* by biochemist Richard Passwater and *Psychodietetics* by E. Cheraskin, M.D., W. M. Ringsdorf, M.D., and Arlene Brecher.

I am of the belief that high-quality natural vitamins are the best. There are trace elements in nature that just cannot be duplicated, so if at all possible, purchase a natural brand. However, even more important is the proper assimilation of your vitamins; there's no point in taking vitamins if your body can't use them. Synthetic or natural, make sure that your vitamins contain no sugar, starch, or preservatives that might hinder your body's utilization of them. Good vitamins are not inexpensive, but because you have eliminated the high cost of red meat, junk foods, sugar, and coffee from your diet, you will still be saving money.

When you are trying to lose weight, take a sugar- and starch-free multivitamin-mineral supplement with your breakfast. As you will be restricting your calorie intake, a low-potency multivitamin that contains the Recommended Daily Allowance of all the vitamins will ensure against depletion.

A WONDER NUTRIENT FOR YOUR FIGURE (AND YOUR NERVES)

Now that you are well on the way to being cellulite- and bloat-free forever, I want to tell you about a marvelous vitamin that will help you attain the svelte shape you are striving for. It is Vitamin B_6, and it is a safe, natural diuretic that also acts as a mood stabilizer. Dr. Carleton Fredericks, many other researchers, and several medical practitioners I know personally have been working with this wonder nutrient since the 1940s and have found that the female hormone estrogen (and the birth control pill) actually destroys B_6 at the time of the month when we need it most. Nutritionally oriented doctors are treating patients suffering from premenstrual tension, water weight, poor skin, and depression with large amounts of Vitamin B_6, and many report that the symptoms disappear almost immediately. I myself suffered from premenstrual tension for years, but no longer since I began taking 3 grams (about 3000 mg) of B_6 daily. One month I ran out of it, and sure enough, the cramps and bloating returned.

For a cellulite condition, I recommend it highly, and several hundred former students who used it reported that it works quickly and effectively.

For the treatment of cellulite and water retention (and fully 90 percent of my students have suffered from one or the other) I recommend 300–600 mg of Vitamin B_6 daily, plus 150–300 mg of Vitamin B complex. B complex should be taken along with B_6 so that you do not create a vitamin imbalance, according to megavitamin specialist Peter Andrus, M.D. Dr. Andrus

35

has assured me that these Vitamin B and B$_6$ levels are safe because B vitamins are water-soluble, so even if you take more than you need (which is unlikely), your body will excrete the excess. Since Vitamin B is destroyed even in many of our fresh foods (they do not generally come direct from the garden to us), it is smart nutritional insurance to take these skin-beautifying, mood-stabilizing supplements.

Experiment with the dosages recommended above to find your best level—begin with the lower dosage and work up to the higher, if necessary. You will know you have reached your best level when you no longer suffer from fluid retention, even before your period, and your cellulite is improving visibly.

B$_6$ is also useful in fighting stress, which I consider to be the biggest health and beauty hazard today. In 1970 Dr. George Goodheart, D.C., the father of applied kinesiology, discovered a connection between the front and back neck muscles, and B$_6$ and niacin amide, in controlled situations. Stress affects all the muscles and organs of the body, particularly the neck, and other doctors, including my associate Dr. Thomas Marchitto, have found that B$_6$ balances the strength of the neck muscles and in so doing, relaxes them. If you have a great deal of stress in your life, you should definitely try to include B$_6$ in your vitamin program.

STAY YOUNGER AND HEALTHIER WITH VITAMIN C

I am very aware of all the publicity—positive and negative—surrounding Vitamin C. I am also aware that very large dosages of Vitamin C have proved to be detrimental in some cases. However, through research, observation, and experimentation with this vitamin, I believe that Vitamin C is one of the most valuable aids we have today in the preservation of health and beauty. In my work as a beauty consultant I have come across many women with bleeding gums, broken capillaries, prematurely aging skin, and varicosities, beauty and health problems that indicate a probable Vitamin C deficiency. Whenever the body is under stress, the need for Vitamin C increases. Alcohol, tobacco, and caffeine as well as stress can nullify the effects of Vitamin C. Because we are exposed to so many pollutants in our atmosphere and in our food, and because we all lead such high-pressure lives, I believe that, as with Vitamin B, it makes sense to take a moderate amount of Vitamin C three times daily, with your other supplements. Experience has proved to me that "Vitamin C people" do indeed exhibit a higher resistance to stress, infection, and prematurely aging skin. Bleeding gums and broken capillaries improve when C is added in judicious amounts. My recommendation is that you take 150 mg of Vitamin C at each meal. I have been assured by nutritionally oriented doctors that this dosage is safe—many of them both take and recommend to their patients much higher dosages. I take 6000 mg of Vitamin C daily, under a doctor's supervision, and I can honestly tell you that I am healthier and less stressed since I added this vitamin, in a high dosage, to my vitamin routine.

DETOXIFY WITH CHLOROPHYLL

Chlorophyll, a natural substance found in plants, has been considered a cleanser and detoxifying agent by health practitioners for thousands of years. Currently, some holistic health facilities are working with it (for example, the Hippocrates Health Institute in Boston) to cure serious diseases. One of my associates, Dr. Thomas Marchitto, D.C., who runs a highly successful chiropractic center in upstate New York, uses it extensively in the treatment of his patients. For our purpose, however, we are concerned with the elimination of cellulite and looking and feeling our best, and chlorophyll has proven valuable as an aid in obtaining optimum beauty and vitality. Several of my students have noticed that they have less of a

problem with breath and body odor after having taken chlorophyll capsules for only a short time. One capsule taken with
your other supplements at mealtime will speed the process of
detoxification, and I do strongly suggest it to you, although it is
not absolutely mandatory on my plan.

Oils for Beauty

Another change that you'll be making in your diet is the addition of cold-pressed vegetable oils and the elimination of all
fried foods and heat-processed oils. Hydrogenated or heated
fats clog the body and do much to promote overweight, cellulite, and poor health generally. On the other hand, pure, light,
minimally processed vegetable oils aid in building a glowing
skin and keeping it wrinkle-free. They also contribute to the
proper distribution of body weight and can actually step up the
burning of hard, stored fat, according to recent studies.

From the standpoint of health, Vitamins A, D, E, and K cannot be assimilated without fat, so oils should be included in
any well-balanced diet, reducing ones included. How many
times have you seen women who crashed-dieted and lost
pounds galore, but whose skin is lifeless, wrinkled, and
lumpy? Chances are that they eliminated fats in the belief that
the more drastic the calorie cut, the better they would look.
Unfortunately, nothing could be further from the truth. A
smooth, glowing skin and shiny, healthy hair are necessary for
true beauty, and the addition of 2 tablespoons of cold-pressed
safflower, sunflower, or other vegetable oil to your daily diet
will help to create and maintain these enviable attributes.

The Good Grains

A most important step toward looking and feeling your best is
the substitution of whole grains for white flour. Whole grains

lose much of their nutritional value in the refining, when the bran and germ are removed. Although in some cases they are "enriched" with a few inexpensive synthetic vitamins and minerals, most of the nutrients are not replaced and the food does not yield the biological value of whole grains. Not only that, but so much sugar, salt, and preservatives are added to white-flour products that the marginal good they offer is often overwhelmed. Beware, too, of "whole-wheat" breads that contain white flour and are colored and flavored to simulate the appearance and taste of whole wheat. These are cheap imitations of the real thing.

Some good, readily available breads that have both taste and health appeal are Branola, Sprouted Wheat, Sprouted Rye, and Bran N' Honey. For special treats, there are many recipes for homemade breads that will win raves from the family. There are even whole-wheat bread mixes available in gourmet shops and health food stores that are quick, easy, and delicious. (Vermont General Store and Grist Mill is one such brand.)

Whole-wheat pasta and long-grain brown rice should be substituted for the white brands. Not only are these foods more delicious, but you will feel fuller more quickly, thus requiring less. Whole-grain rice must simmer longer than the white kind, but aside from that, it requires no additional preparation. Whole-wheat, artichoke, or spinach pasta can be prepared exactly like white pasta and used as a base for casseroles, cheese, and tomato sauces, as well as an exciting entree or an accompaniment to meat or fish.

If you are overweight, or suffer from cellulite, limit your bread, rice, pasta, and potatoes until the undesirable condition is eliminated. Unfortunately, women over thirty develop an increasing inability to handle starchy foods effectively because they tend to cause fluid retention. If you have a tendency to retain fluid, be very sparing with starchy carbohydrates. Experiment by weighing yourself daily, while you adjust your intake to the optimum level for your body. Some women will find that when they add a potato or an extra serving of bread to the basic diet they increase their weight by as much as two pounds in twenty-four hours. If this happens to you, be aware that your system is supersensitive to starch, and modify your intake accordingly.

Those fortunate enough to be cellulite-free and at their perfect weight can enjoy whole-grain bread products with my blessing. Growing children and active men will benefit from these energy foods, too. Whole grains can be the basis for wonderful piecrusts, cakes, and dessert treats. Whole-wheat pastry flour, which can be purchased in most supermarkets, is the whole-grain flour best suited for these purposes.

Brewer's Yeast—the Wonder Food

Every day from now on you are going to increase your energy and well-being with two "beauty breaks." (This is a good substitute for the coffee break.) Brewer's yeast is one of the most beauty-making, energy-giving foods available. In my opinion, it has not become popular because so many forms of it are unpalatable, and because people do not use it properly. After much searching, I have found three brands of brewer's yeast that are virtually tasteless: Red Star Yeast Flakes (not Red Star baker's yeast), Hauser Yeast (developed by Gayelord Hauser), and Lewis Yeast. Make a beauty cocktail by stirring ¼ teaspoon yeast into a 6-ounce can of low-sodium V-8 juice or unsweetened grapefruit juice if you are dieting, or into any unsweetened fruit juice, milk, or yogurt if you are not. After one week, increase the yeast to ½ teaspoon, and continue to increase your intake of yeast by ½ teaspoon twice daily until you are taking a total of 4 tablespoons a day.

Why is it necessary to begin taking brewer's yeast slowly? If your diet has been poor or if you have been taking certain drugs, you may have insufficient intestinal flora. The yeast, while helping to replace beneficial bacteria in the intestinal tract, also will create gas and bloat if too much is taken too soon—certainly not a beautiful condition! However, when it is introduced gradually, it will boost your energy level quickly, improve your skin, act as an appetite depressant and a low-calorie source of complete protein, and help keep you youthful. So much from so little—it is easy to see why brewer's yeast is truly a wonder food.

Yeast is a source of complete protein, and it includes all the elements of the Vitamin B complex, including the trace mineral chromium and nucleic acids, difficult to obtain in many foods, which researchers believe to be important in the preservation of a youthful appearance. Once your system is used to a goodly amount of this protein food, add it to cereals, casseroles, breads, and eggs.

A New Old Beauty Food: Yogurt

Another addition to your new diet is plain yogurt with live cultures. Yogurt is not a new food. It has been used for thousands of years by peoples well known for their longevity, in particular the Bulgarians and the Russians. Yogurt contains Lactobacillus acidophilus, which implants itself in the intestinal tract and helps to prevent constipation, diarrhea, and other intestinal complaints. It is often recommended by physicians to lessen the effects of drugs, especially antibiotics.

I must admit that I was not always a yogurt enthusiast. Quite the opposite. However, I noticed that many of my European students were the proud possessors of gorgeous skin. They had other beauty and weight problems, but their skin was enviable. Naturally, I queried them as to their secrets, and all of them related that at least a cup daily of high-quality yogurt was a staple part of their diet and that they used yogurt externally, too, as a cosmetic. More about the cosmetic uses of yogurt in Week Three; here, suffice it to say that I began to eat yogurt and my skin improved. As I passed this information on to our teachers and students and they began to use it, they reported improved clarity and texture of both face and body skin.

I am happy to see the popularity of yogurt rising, but I must warn you against the presweetened, prefruited, and frozen varieties that abound in supermarkets. They are loaded with sugar and preservatives. Dannon, Breyer's, and Columbo natural plain yogurts are good brands, and many excellent yogurts can be purchased in the health food store. Whatever brand you choose, check to make sure that the label lists active cultures as one of the ingredients.

You can make your own yogurt less expensively from a small amount of a good commercial brand and low-fat milk. Yogurt need not be eaten plain if you don't like the taste; my diet plan includes a delicious yogurt instant meal, which I hope you will try.

Yogurt can be substituted for sour cream or mayonnaise, or for fattening puddings (add a natural flavor extract like banana, almond, orange, or vanilla to plain yogurt). It is a delicious addition to stews and sauces, and can even be used as a pie filling. Although I highly recommend yogurt for beauty and health, if you cannot abide it, it is not absolutely necessary, unlike spring water and yeast. Remember, this diet is to be a pleasure, not a sacrifice.

Beauty and Energy for the Rest of Your Life

Today is the first day of a new, delightful way of life. Did you know that in a single year 98 percent of the atoms making up your body will be replaced by new ones? You can completely rebuild yourself into the beautiful, vibrant person you were meant to be. Beauty and health are up to you.

L-glutamine can reduce your craving for sweets; Vitamin B₆ taken along with the entire B complex will improve your figure and your mood; Vitamin C will beautify your skin and help prevent premature aging; and chlorophyll capsules will speed the elimination of all your "past sins" (preservatives, sugar, and the like) from your body. Always take these supplements with meals. With these supplements, you should suffer no feelings of deprivation. Adequate protein will help keep your blood sugar level stable, and spring water will cleanse the tissues, organs, and skin of cellulite and accumulated toxins.

A Week's Worth of Exercise

As you begin the Over-30 Diet, I also want you to warm up for next week's Body Sculpting regime. That regime, which will help you have the figure you've always dreamed of having, is very rigorous, and so right now you must begin to loosen and limber your muscles and increase your endurance.

From now on, be very conscious of your breathing, especially when you are exercising. Often we breathe incorrectly or shallowly due to tension, negative emotion, or poor posture. Circulation is constricted, muscles tense, and the body tightens. Break this vicious circle and begin to breathe and move joyfully, freely, and youthfully. As you begin to exercise and remove the kinks, breathe consciously and audibly with each movement. By breathing correctly, you increase the efficacy of your exercises.

The Body Twist will limber all your muscles and help get them in shape for the workout ahead. You need to perform this exercise this week only. I also want you to do two other warm-up exercises, which you will continue to do next week when you start your Body Sculpting program. Wall Bends and the Spine Stretch are both excellent exercises to promote flexibility.

43

The Body Twist

Practice very slowly at first, concentrating on the correct movements, your breathing, and the stretch. Within a day or so you will be able to perform it rapidly and rhythmically.

1   Stand tall, facing a full-length mirror, feet shoulder width apart and pointed straight ahead, arms out at the sides at shoulder level, palms turned down. Flex the knees slightly.

2   S-t-r-e-t-c-h your arms to the side, twist the upper body to the left as far as possible (to the point of strain, not pain), and inhale.

3 Exhale as you try to touch your right palm to the floor (do the best you can).

4 Inhale as you straighten up with your upper body still twisted.

5 Exhale as you return to your original position.

6 Repeat exercise on the opposite side. The first three days of this week, do 10 repetitions daily; do 20 repetitions for the next four days.

Wall Bends

Maintain a smooth, rhythmic motion throughout this exercise. After you complete it, take a few moments to observe the new flow of warmth and energy in your body.

1 Stand tall, feet shoulder width apart, heels 12 inches away from a wall.

2 Raise your arms overhead, stretch backward, and touch your fingertips to the wall as you inhale.

3 Exhale, bend forward from the waist, and try to touch your toes. Do 20 repetitions per day, this week.

The Spine Stretch

1 Stand tall and place your hands on your hips.

2 Stretch your right arm up toward the ceiling. Look up at your right hand as you inhale.

3 Exhale and return hand to hip. Repeat 10 times.

4 Stretch to the left 10 times.

The Over-30 Diet

This is the diet that has worked for hundreds of my students, helping them to lose weight quickly and painlessly, diminish their cellulite, rejuvenate their skin, and make their energy level rise. If you are overweight, stick to the Basic Diet until you have lost the weight you wish, and then enjoy the maintenance variations at the end of each meal. Maintaining weight loss, as I will discuss further in Week Six, is the hardest part of any diet. Unfortunately, for the over-thirty woman the difference between maintaining weight and putting on unwanted pounds is very small indeed.

I have also included variations on the Basic Diet for the underweight woman. Although they are in the minority, underweight women suffer as much with their problem as do overweight women, especially over thirty. After thirty, the youthful layer of fatty tissue underneath the skin begins to thin out, accentuating a bony woman's frame even more. Many underweight women, in a desperate attempt to gain weight, resort to gorging themselves on sweets and junk foods. The body, malnourished and insulted, stubbornly refuses to add pounds, but instead accumulates all sorts of skin problems, from breakouts to under-eye circles and cellulite. (Remember, cellulite is *not* fat, and can be as much of a problem for thin women as for the overweight.) My diet adds calories in the form of starches, whole grains, nuts, seeds, fruit, whole milk, and honey—all of which are beauty- and health-making foods that will nourish and sustain the body as well as add pounds. The weight-gain suggestions at the end of each meal can also be used for children in your family, or for men, who require a higher calorie intake.

Two excellent cookbooks that contain luscious recipes for

the whole family are Beatrice Trum Hunter's *Natural Foods Cookbook* and Francine Prince's *Dieter's Gourmet Cookbook*. After you have stabilized your weight and learned to make healthful eating a daily habit, I suggest you try serving your friends and loved ones some of the wonderful nutritious treats contained in these books.

Now, on to breakfast!

BEFORE BREAKFAST, EVERY MORNING

Squeeze the juice of half a fresh lemon into 4 ounces of hot spring water. Drink this when you wake up—it will act as a mild detoxifying agent, diuretic, and laxative, and help to clarify the complexion.

Basic Breakfast

A good breakfast is vital to beauty and health and should contain at least one-fourth of your total daily protein intake. Here are four different breakfasts to choose from, all delicious and filling, so that no matter how much or how little time you have in the morning you will have no excuse to skip breakfast. An instant breakfast takes just a minute to make and can be sipped as you prepare for your day. In fact, either of the instant meals can be substituted at any time for lunch or dinner if you are on the run and do not have time for a more leisurely meal.

1 *Instant Beauty Breakfast.* Whiz in your blender, at high speed for 60 seconds, the following ingredients: 6 ounces unsweetened orange juice (or, better yet, the juice of 2 freshly squeezed oranges) or unfiltered, unsweetened apple juice, 1 raw egg, 2 tablespoons non-fat dry milk powder, 1 tablespoon protein powder (NOTE: When shopping for protein powder, look on the container for a protein efficiency ration, or PER, of 2.5. This assures you of high quality), and 2 ice cubes made of spring water. Sip slowly through a straw.

2 *Instant Yogurt Breakfast.* Blend together 1½ cups plain yogurt (make sure it contains active cultures), 2 tablespoons nonfat dry milk powder, ¼ teaspoon raw honey, 1 peach or nectarine or 3 tablespoons unsweetened crushed pineapple or 10 strawberries or ½ cup blueberries, and 2 ice cubes made of spring water.
NOTE: Interesting variations on this instant meal can be made by using half portions of different fruits—peaches and blueberries make a delicious combination, for instance.

3 ½ cup fresh orange or grapefruit slices, 1 slice whole-grain toast with 1 pat unsalted butter, and 1 egg, poached, boiled, or scrambled with 2 tablespoons low-fat milk in a nonstick pan. Garnish with freshly ground black pepper and chives.
NOTE: To make a nutritious soft butter (commercial soft margarine contains too many additives and colorings, in addition to salt) combine ½ cup safflower or sunflower oil with ½ cup unsalted butter. Delicious!

4 ½ grapefruit and 1 slice whole-grain toast topped with a thin layer of unprocessed mild cheese. Add a thin layer of sliced tomato if you wish, and broil until the cheese bubbles.

★ **Don't forget your supplements:** 1 multivitamin capsule, Vitamin B, Vitamin B$_6$, Vitamin C, and 1 chlorophyll capsule.

Maintenance Breakfast Variations

To breakfasts #1, 2, and 3, add 1 slice whole-grain toast, lightly buttered. To breakfast #4, add tablespoons water-packed white meat tuna to tomato and cheese.

Or enjoy a fruit-and-cereal-lover's breakfast of ⅓ cup Swiss Muesli (found in health food stores and gourmet shops) combined with 1 diced apple and ½ cup plain yogurt or low-fat milk.

Weight-Gain Breakfast Variations

Make a higher-calorie meal by adding a banana to the Instant Beauty Breakfast, or substitute a banana for some of the fruit in the Instant Yogurt Breakfast, increasing the yogurt to 1 cup and adding honey to taste. Eat 2 buttered bran, whole-wheat, or corn muffins with breakfast.

Or have 2 eggs, scrambled with whole milk and grated cheese, 2 slices buttered whole-wheat toast, and ½ grapefruit.

Or 1 cup granola cereal mixed with 1 sliced banana and ¾ cup yogurt.

BASIC MIDMORNING BEAUTY BREAK

Stir ¼ teaspoon brewer's yeast into 6 ounces low-sodium V-8 juice or unsweetened grapefruit juice. Increase yeast intake as previously directed.

Maintenance Variation
Substitute 6 ounces of any unsweetened fruit juice.

Basic Lunch

The basis for this meal is a fresh, beautiful salad. If you are a working woman eating at your desk, seal your vegetables in an airtight container and store them in a cool place until you are ready to eat. Many restaurants today have salad bars, so dining out should not be a problem. If you are a homemaker, chop up the vegetables as close to lunchtime as possible, for optimum nutrition. Be imaginative—combine fresh sliced mushrooms with sliced zucchini, add raw green beans and broccoli, or cabbage and carrots, bell pepper, Spanish onion, cherry tomatoes, radishes, scallions, celery, raw sprouts, beets, or raw spinach to any dark, leafy greens.

Add 3 ounces of protein food to the salad: shrimp, lobster, crabmeat, flaked white tuna (water-packed), cooked fish fillet, unprocessed chicken or turkey, or chopped hard-cooked egg. Or you can add ½ cup cottage cheese or 1½ ounces hard cheese.

Toss the protein of your choice with the vegetables and 1½ tablespoons Basic Salad Dressing.

51

BASIC SALAD DRESSING

¾ cup cold-pressed safflower or sunflower oil
*¼ cup natural apple cider vinegar or fresh lemon juice freshly
ground black pepper*
1–1½ teaspoons dried herbs (for example, tarragon, basil, or dill)
Optional: *1 clove garlic (minced for stronger flavor; split and removed after 2 hours for less)*

Put all ingredients in a jar, shake vigorously, and refrigerate.

⋆**Don't forget your supplements:** Vitamin B, Vitamin B$_6$, Vitamin C, and 1
chlorophyll capsule.

Maintenance Lunch Variation

Add 1 slice whole-wheat bread or 1 small whole-wheat roll, lightly
buttered.

Weight-Gain Lunch Variation

Add up to 6 ounces of protein food to salad, along with cold
chopped potatoes or whole-wheat pasta if desired. Toss with 3
tablespoons Basic Salad Dressing. Eat 1 or 2 slices buttered whole-
wheat bread or rolls, and finish with a fruit dessert made with honey
or 2 ounces dessert cheese (Brie, Port Salut, or Camembert) with
unsalted whole-wheat crackers and 1 serving fresh fruit (grapes,
cherries, bananas).

MIDAFTERNOON BEAUTY BREAK

Same as midmorning.

Basic Dinner

Start off with a small vegetable salad tossed with 1 tablespoon
Basic Salad Dressing. The enzymes produced by the raw foods
will be activated and help you digest your other nutrients
better.

Follow the salad with 2 fresh steamed vegetables (up to 1 cup of each), one of which is either broccoli or asparagus. Broccoli and asparagus are natural diuretics that help the body rid itself of excess fluids (especially important for cellulite sufferers). Avoid corn, lima beans, and peas. Dress the vegetables with herbs and lemon juice, or dot sparingly with unsalted butter.

To steam vegetables properly, put washed and cut-up vegetables in a steamer basket (available for about four dollars in any department store). Add one inch of water to the bottom of a pan and put the steamer basket in it; the water should not touch the vegetables. Cover the pan tightly and turn the stove to high. Reduce the heat when the water comes to a rolling boil, and steam until the vegetables turn a *bright* color—no longer!

Be inventive with your combinations of fresh vegetables, and vary them daily. For example, zucchini, eggplant, and squash combine well with tomatoes, onions, and green peppers. Peas and carrots are a classic team. Spinach and beets make a luscious combination. (Steaming times for vegetables do vary, so steam them separately and combine when you serve.) The secret to enjoying these foods is to get the finest-quality produce you can find. Make sure to cut up the vegetables as close to mealtime as possible. When they are properly cooked, they will be crunchy and much more flavorful than the mushy canned and frozen ones.

Next on our dinner menu is a delicious entree of up to ⅓ pound of fish, chicken, turkey, or veal, which can be baked, broiled, or boiled, but not fried. Experiment with herbs and other seasonings; the imaginative use of them is a quick and low-calorie way to transform plain meat or fish into a special dish. Tarragon and lemon juice sprinkled on a chicken breast before baking enhances its flavor tremendously, for instance. Fish broiled with chopped parsley and scallions and a dash of white wine is delicious. (For cooking purposes, I allow my students to use a small amount of dry white wine—it enhances the flavor of many dishes and adds very few calories.)

I believe strongly that it is wise to give the system a rest from meat and fish for one complete meal a week. The beauty and health benefits are well worth it. Here is a recipe for an absolutely delicious, filling, quick-to-prepare vegetarian dish, which can be substituted on this diet at any time for a meat or fish entree. Make sure that you enjoy it at least once a week.

ELIZABETH'S VEGETABLE QUICHE

4 eggs
½ cup low-fat milk fortified with 2 tablespoons nonfat dry milk powder
black pepper to taste
1 cup fresh mushrooms, washed and sliced thin
1 cup fresh spinach, washed and torn into small pieces
4 ounces unprocessed mild cheese, sliced very thin
dash of nutmeg

Lightly grease the bottom of a small round baking dish. Beat eggs, milk, and pepper until frothy and mixed thoroughly. Layer mushrooms in the bottom of the pan, then the spinach pieces and cheese slices. Pour egg mixture over all. Sprinkle with nutmeg. Cover dish and bake at 425° F. until quiche puffs up and top acquires a light brown crust. Do not overcook! *Makes 2 servings.*

NOTE: Vegetables used may vary. In place of mushrooms and spinach, try tomatoes and thin strips of broccoli or asparagus, for example.

★**Don't forget your supplements:** Vitamin B, Vitamin B$_6$, Vitamin C, and 1 chlorophyll capsule.

Maintenance Dinner Variation

Add 1 medium baked potato garnished with yogurt and chives, or ½ cup whole-wheat pasta or brown rice. Finish with fresh fruit (try ½ broiled grapefruit, ⅛ honeydew melon, or ½ frozen banana).

Weight-Gain Dinner Variation

Have as much salad as you wish; garnish fruit salad with walnuts, flaked coconut, and sunflower seeds. Increase meat or fish allowance to ½ pound. Add 1-cup serving of whole-wheat pasta or brown rice, and have whole-wheat bread or rolls if desired. Finish meal with a natural fruit dessert made with honey, or ice cream made with honey (Häagen-Dazs makes a delicious carob ice cream sweetened with honey instead of sugar). At bedtime, drink 1 cup hot whole milk into which 1 tablespoon blackstrap molasses has been stirred.

On your meatless day, have a large portion of Elizabeth's Vegetable Quiche, but made with whole milk rather than skim, topped with wheat germ, and baked in a whole-wheat pastry shell (preservative-free pastry shells can be found in the frozen food departments of most large supermarkets, or you can make your own easily).

Remember to drink 8 glasses of spring water during the day and evening. Sip slowly. Do not eat and drink at the same time, except for a few swallows of water with your supplements.

Bon appetit!

Week Two

The Body Sculpting Program

FOR one full week now, you have been on the Over-30 Diet. You have chosen the variation that best fits your needs, and within the next week, if you haven't felt it already, you will notice a definite improvement in your energy level, your cellulite will begin to diminish, your skin and eyes will glow, little lines and wrinkles will be minimized, and you will actually begin to look younger. I'm sure that your body is already more youthful-looking and curvier, because you've lost a lot of the bloat that preservatives and salt create in the areas of waist, abdomen, knees, and ankles.

You have also begun to prepare your body for a new exercise regime. You have practiced the Body Twist daily and have learned other warm-up stretches too. During the next week, you will be working up to your optimum number of repetitions of the Body Sculpting exercises best suited to your needs, and settling into an exercise routine at a time convenient for you.

I want you to understand clearly that this exercise program has been specifically designed for women 10 to 25 pounds overweight, women who are underweight, those of correct weight who wish to become better proportioned, and those who suffer from cellulite. If you are extremely overweight, or have back problems or any other physical problem that would be aggravated by strenuous exercise, *do not attempt this regime except upon the advice of your physician.*

The purpose of Body Sculpting is to help you achieve the

beautiful figure you were meant to have. It is not meant to be a substitute for athletic or endurance exercise (jumping rope, walking, swimming, aerobic dancing, etc.), although certainly it will increase your endurance. Speaking of endurance exercise, as an exercise specialist I truly believe that walking and swimming are the two finest rejuvenating and strengthening exercises for women over thirty. I don't like to see women with heavy legs or cellulite jogging, jumping rope, or performing strenuous dance routines. I have had many students who, before they came to me, jogged or danced their way into such a hard cellulite condition, or into such muscular legs, that it took twice as long as usual to undo the damage. I do not recommend weight training, either, for a woman with heavy legs. Weights will build muscle and firm up the fat—*not* get rid of fat, as is so often mistakenly believed. Far better to first get rid of the flab and then, if muscle definition is indicated, begin a weight program.

In addition to Body Sculpting, if possible incorporate this walking routine, which I call the Cross Crawl, into your day (one to three miles, if possible):

Walk briskly with long strides, inhaling deeply to the count of 4 steps, then exhaling fully to the count of 4 steps. Make sure that your arms swing vigorously as you walk, matching your arm with your opposite leg.

In the beginning, you may feel slightly weak or breathless as your body accustoms itself to the accelerated intake of oxygen. Within a week, however, you will feel more energetic throughout the day. Your skin will acquire an added sheen, and your body skin will begin to glow with a youthful luster that is the result of your improved circulation.

This exercise can truly become a "positive addiction." Do it as soon as you arise. I'll bet that no matter how early you have to get up, you'll soon (like me) awaken a half hour earlier in order to accommodate this delightful habit!

Before we begin, let me tell you a little about how this

program evolved. I've already mentioned my own experience with physical culture, and how I completely reproportioned my figure in three months. When I joined the teaching staff of the modeling agency school, I immediately began to study and experiment with different experts' exercise techniques, along with the techniques I had already learned. After seventeen years of teaching, I have developed, I firmly believe, one of the fastest and most effective exercise programs available. It can be done anywhere, without equipment (except for 3-pound weights), and without any additional strain on your budget. Sound too good to be true? Read on.

My first students were aspiring models. Contrary to popular opinion, models are made, not born. Those who succeed are those who are willing to correct their flaws, and nowhere is this more important than in the area of figure, which must be perfect for the purpose of displaying clothes to their best advantage. Models are highly motivated to acquire and keep ideal proportions, because their livelihood depends on it. The models who were my students were willing to follow my directions and perform the high number of repetitions that I required, and the results they achieved were often nothing short of spectacular. Hips disappeared, cellulite vanished, heavy legs became shapely, waistlines were whittled, and breasts became larger in some cases, firmer in others. What made me (and the models) so happy was that the transformation was very rapid.

My subsequent students, active over-thirty women of all professions and lifestyles, were not in search of perfection, but they cared enough about themselves to put forth the effort necessary to become their very best. When they followed my directions, they too were rewarded with dramatic changes in their figures. So, too, it will be with you, *if you are willing to work at it.*

This will be the most difficult week of the program. You

must not skip days, and you must discipline yourself to perform high repetitions of each exercise. If you have been sedentary in the past, you will be sore for a few days, but this will pass. I do not ever want you to hurt yourself, and pain is not the same as soreness. I'm sure you know the difference. Accept the soreness, and realize that it is only temporary. Each evening, relax in a warm tub, and in a few days the soreness will be nothing more than a memory. The first few days, too, you will spend more time on your exercises as you work to establish correct breathing and performance patterns. Ride it out. Soon you will flow easily from one exercise to the next.

Why must you do so many repetitions to achieve results? In order to acquire something, you must work at it. I have taught many women who came to me as a last resort. They had tried gimmicks, spas, machines, pills, creams, and sports in the hope of improving their figure problems. The methods failed, or the results were so slow in coming that the women lost incentive. After only a week on my program, their bodies showed definite improvement. Spurred on by their initial success, these women continued diligently to follow the program, and the results they had so long desired were achieved in short order. They worked at it and they were rewarded. There is no magic pill, no shortcut, no effortless way to get in great shape fast except with high repetitions. The only other "instant" fitness program that I have found to be effective is the Nautilus program, which is very strenuous but good. If you want to achieve fast, optimum results, follow my instructions to the letter. Do not fool yourself into thinking that a few exercises performed halfheartedly will achieve any noticeable results. They won't.

If you are a real exercise buff and in search of absolute perfection, as were my very first students, I strongly suggest that you double the routine that best suits your needs. You will see incredibly fast results, and, in my opinion, will be much more inclined to follow the entire program for a lifetime when you see the perfect figure you've always wanted become a reality.

I know that most of you are not willing to spend the amount of time necessary for such a concentrated routine, but I am confident that high repetitions will result in the sculpting of a figure that you will be most happy to claim as your own.

A current student of mine, a young psychologist, came to me because her once perfect figure had gone to ruin and cellulite was blossoming from her derriere to her ankles. At thirty years of age, she was frightened because "if I look like this now, what will I be at forty?" At our first meeting I charted a set of ideal measurements for her and advised her as to a diet that would cleanse her system, clear her skin, help dissolve her cellulite, and improve her energy level. In one week she returned, noticeably less bloated, feeling better and more energetic. She was given an individualized, high-repetition exercise program that emphasized the legs (her worst feature). Two weeks later, she returned for more direction, happy and full of energy. I measured her and immediately knew that she was neglecting her leg exercises; the measurements were only slightly smaller. "But," she complained, "I'm doing so well on my diet . . . all my friends have complimented me on my appearance . . . why do I have to do all those boring repetitions?" "Because," I told her, "your biggest problem area is your legs, and even though you will lose weight and gain energy and beauty with attention to diet, your saddlebags will stay flabby and unsightly unless you work them off with Thigh and Calf Slaps." Well, I must have convinced her, because now, only two months later, she has lost a total of 6 inches in her thighs, with only 1½ inches to go before she reaches her best proportions. She is looking forward to wearing a skimpy bikini when she vacations in Florida this spring. Had she not diligently applied herself to the exercise program, the bikini would be nothing more than a daydream.

Perhaps there are some skeptics among you who say that we must live with what we were born with, and that hereditary tendencies rule the destiny of our figures. To that argument I say, "Rubbish!" That's a good excuse for remaining forever inactive. Of course we cannot change our bone structure—we are small-, medium-, or large-boned. However, we can change our proportions and our tendencies—with effort. For example, suppose your hips and legs are heavy. It's not because your bones are heavy, but because your weight is proportioned incorrectly, with the emphasis on the bottom. I've never seen a woman whose hip bones were wider than her shoulders, but I've seen many a heavy-hipped person who, with attention to the correct exercises, achieved hips slim enough to be proudly displayed in even the tightest of jeans. Improper distribution of fat is not hereditary and can be corrected.

Another old wives' tale that should go the way of the winds is the "I'm just getting older, it's natural to be flabby (fat, veiny, wrinkly . . . whatever)." Quite the opposite! Most other cultures believe that as a woman ages she becomes more beautiful. It's about time that we began to make this belief fact in our culture, too. It is natural to function at peak performance and to maintain a beautiful body from young adulthood until nearly the end of a lifetime. Consider the development of all other living creatures. Their appearance, vitality, and flexibility remain virtually the same until the very end of life. Can you really tell the difference between a seven-year-old animal and a two-year-old animal? Why, then, do we humans seem to age at a more accelerated rate? Because of poor dietary habits, not enough physical exercise, poor posture, and too much tension. Have you ever seen an animal sit all day without moving or stretching? Plenty of humans do! Most of the abuse we heap upon ourselves without thinking is the result of our self-indulgent and sedentary way of life.

Without any further discussion, I'd like to begin right now to help you become your most curvaceous self.

The First Step: A Personal Body Analysis

Before you actually begin to exercise, take completely objective and precise stock of your body. "Know yourself objectively" is my dictum—for if you aren't honest with yourself, how can you ever expect to improve?

For this self-knowledge, you will need a piece of paper (or use the chart provided in the Appendix) and a pencil, a tape measure, a full-length mirror, and a few minutes of uninterrupted quiet. Remove all constricting garments (if you own a leotard and tights, put them on) and stand full face in front of the mirror. Let your body relax completely (do not hold your stomach in!) and take visual note, first, of the areas you would like to improve. Next, looking straight into the mirror, take your measurements and record them.

BUST

Circle the back and breasts at the largest point around—make sure the tape measure is absolutely straight. Hold it so that you do not "squish" the delicate breast tissue.

WAIST

Bring the tape measure down around the smallest part of your *relaxed* waistline. (Do not cheat; you would only be cheating yourself.) The tape measure should be taut, but relaxed enough so that one finger can fit between it and your waist.

ABDOMEN OR UPPER HIP

Locate your hip bones (the bones on either side of your navel). Relax your abdomen and circle this area straight all around with the tape measure.

LOWER HIP

Locate the fullest part of the derriere and bring the tape straight around this area.

THIGH

Stand with knees straight. Locate the fleshiest portion of your thigh and circle the area straight around (do not let the tape ride up). The tape should be taut, but relaxed enough so you can slide one finger comfortably between it and your leg.

You may wish to measure both thighs. Usually, the right thigh will be slightly larger than the left, in some cases by an inch or more. It is possible to even out the thighs with exercise.

KNEE

Stand with a straight leg. Measure the knee just above the bone.

CALF

Stand with a straight leg. Measure the calf around the fullest part of the calf muscle.

ANKLE

Measure the ankle just above the ankle bone.

Each week from now on, on the same day, take all these measurements exactly as you did today. Weekly measurement taking will become part of your lifestyle. It will keep you on the right track and alert to any possible problems for the rest of your life.

The curves between waist and bust and waist and hips are

what the eye perceives as a truly feminine figure. For this reason, I believe that there ideally should be a 12-inch (not 10-inch) difference between the bust and the waist. The upper hip should be 2 to 3 inches smaller than the lower hip. This area is what gives the female body its roundness.

The bust and hips should measure approximately the same, with 1-inch deviation either way possible. The thighs should measure no more than 21 inches around, even on a tall, large-boned woman, nor less than 18 inches even for a petite, small-boned frame. The knee should be approximately 6 inches smaller than the thigh, the calf 7 inches smaller than the thigh, and the ankle approximately 4½ to 5 inches smaller than the calf. Determine your ideal measurements and record them.

The Body Sculpting Regime

Look in the mirror with a constructively critical eye. What figure tendencies do you possess? Many women tend to carry weight in the lower half of the body. The bust is relatively small, the arms are slender, the abdomen is fairly flat. Then the trouble starts! Hips, thighs, and frequently knees and lower legs, too, carry the majority of fat.

Other women have the opposite problem: heavy arms, bust, waist, and abdominal areas. Generally these women have slim hips and legs.

A third common figure type is the boyish, slim, straight, and undeveloped female figure. This type can be just as distressing to its owner as the too-generous form.

Sometimes I also see a well-proportioned figure "gone to pot": Although bust, hips, and waist are in good proportion, the arms, abdomen, derriere, and legs are flabby.

Finally, athletic women have problems too: Often the waist is poorly defined, and the legs are too muscular (often combined with a hard cellulite condition).

I have designed an exercise program for each figure type. Although the majority of you will undoubtedly identify with one of them, at the conclusion of each exercise I also recommend numbers of repetitions for specific problems, so that if you have only one or two areas to improve, you can tailor the exercises to your specific needs. A good rule of thumb is to concentrate *at least 60 percent* of your workout on the problem areas that trouble you most.

1 Heavy hips and legs; small bust

Stretches: 10 repetitions each

DAILY

FOR THE LEGS, HIPS, AND DERRIERE
Thigh Slaps: 150–200 repetitions, each side
Calf Slaps: 150–200 repetitions, each side
Leg Lifts: 2 sets of 10 repetitions, each side
Leg Circles: 2 sets of 10 repetitions, each side
Bottom Shapers: 3 sets of 10 repetitions, each side
Side Lunges: 2 sets of 10 repetitions, each side

FOR THE WAIST
Waist Bends: 25 repetitions, each side

FOR THE ABDOMEN
Bench Sit-ups: 15 repetitions

EVERY OTHER DAY
FOR THE BUST
Flys: 3 sets of 10 repetitions
Bench Press: 3 sets of 10 repetitions
Pullovers: 3 sets of 10 repetitions

2 Slim hips and legs; heavy bust, waist, and arms

Stretches: 10 repetitions each

DAILY

FOR THE LEGS, HIPS, AND DERRIERE
Thigh Slaps: 50 repetitions, each side
Leg Lifts: 10 repetitions, each side
Leg Circles: 10 repetitions, each side

Bottom Shapers: 10 repetitions, each side
Double Kickbacks: 10 repetitions, each side
Side Lunges: 10 repetitions, each side

FOR THE WAIST
Waist Bends: 75–100 repetitions, each side
Waist Twists: 50 rotations

FOR THE ABDOMEN
Bench Sit-ups: 20–25 repetitions
Jackknives: 20–25 repetitions

EVERY OTHER DAY
FOR THE BUST
Bench Press: 3 sets of 10 repetitions
Pullovers: 3 sets of 10 repetitions
Arm Circles: 3 sets of 10 revolutions

NOTE: If the long muscle in the front of the thigh is underdeveloped, add Squats: 2 sets of 10 repetitions with weights, every other day.

3 Too-slim, straight-up-and-down figure

Stretches: 10 repetitions each

DAILY
FOR THE LEGS, HIPS, AND DERRIERE
Thigh Slaps: 25 repetitions, each side
Leg Lifts: 2 sets of 10 repetitions, each side
Leg Circles: 2 sets of 10 repetitions, each side
Bottom Shapers: 3 sets of 10 repetitions, each side
Side Lunges: 10 repetitions, each side
Squats: 3 sets of 10 repetitions

FOR THE WAIST
Waist Bends: 100 repetitions, each side
Waist Twists: 75 rotations

FOR THE ABDOMEN
Bench Sit-ups: 10 repetitions
Jackknives: 10 repetitions

EVERY OTHER DAY
FOR THE BUST
Flys: 3 sets of 10 repetitions
Bench Press: 3 sets of 10 repetitions
Pullovers: 3 sets of 10 repetitions
Arm Circles: 3 sets of 10 revolutions

4 Well-proportioned hips, waist, and bust; flabby abdomen, derriere, and legs

Stretches: 10 repetitions each

DAILY
FOR THE LEGS, HIPS, AND DERRIERE
Thigh Slaps: 100–200 repetitions, each side
Calf Slaps: 100–200 repetitions, each side
Leg Lifts: 2 sets of 10 repetitions, each side
Bottom Shapers: 2 sets of 10 repetitions, each side
Double Kickbacks: 2 sets of 10 repetitions, each side
Side Lunges: 2 sets of 10 repetitions, each side
Squats: 2 sets of 10 repetitions (if muscle definition is desired)

FOR THE WAIST
Waist Bends: 25 repetitions, each side

FOR THE ABDOMEN
Bench Sit-ups: 25 repetitions
Jackknives: 20 repetitions

EVERY OTHER DAY
FOR THE BUST
Pullovers: 2 sets of 10 repetitions
Arm Circles: 2 sets of 10 revolutions

5 Athletic build, with thick waist and over-developed legs

Stretches: 10 repetitions each

DAILY
FOR THE LEGS, HIPS, AND DERRIERE
Thigh Slaps: 75–150 repetitions, each side
Calf Slaps: 100–200 repetitions, each side
Leg Lifts: 10 repetitions, each side
Leg Circles: 10 repetitions, each side
Double Kickbacks: 10 repetitions, each side

FOR THE WAIST
Waist Bends: 100 repetitions, each side
Waist Twists: 50 rotations

FOR THE ABDOMEN
Bench Sit-ups: 20 repetitions

EVERY OTHER DAY
FOR THE BUST
Flys: 3 sets of 10 repetitions
Bench Press: 3 sets of 10 repetitions
Pullovers: 3 sets of 10 repetitions

FOR THE LEGS, HIPS, AND DERRIERE

The Thigh Slap

This is the *single most effective exercise* I have ever found for reducing hips and getting rid of the dreadful saddlebag thighs that are the bane of many women. It is the "magic" exercise that has literally melted fat and cellulite from my students. One cautionary note: Be sure that the floor is covered with a rug or blanket and that you are wearing tights or loose pants to prevent bruises and broken blood vessels. Do not be afraid to slap hard, however; you will not hurt yourself. If you do see an occasional black-and-blue mark on the side of the knee, simply tape a piece of cotton to it before you exercise. Another tip: If you "scooch" along the floor too much during this exercise, wear sneakers.

1 Sit on the floor with your knees bent, ankles touching. Try to keep your heels as close to your derriere as possible. Your arms should be behind you, elbows slightly bent, palms flat on the floor.

2 Keep your upper body straight as you twist your hips to the right and slap your right thigh hard on the floor. The slap should be audible, and you should feel it!

3 Twist your lower body to the left and slap your left thigh hard on the floor, keeping your knees and ankles together.

RECOMMENDED REPETITIONS

For cellulite sufferers, or for saddlebag thighs: 150–200 repetitions, each side

For hips 2–3 inches out of proportion: 100–200 repetitions, each side

For hipline maintenance: 50 repetitions, each side

70

FOR THE LEGS, HIPS, AND DERRIERE

The Calf Slap

Here's another magic leg exercise that will help rid the back of your legs of those unsightly cellulite deposits, excess fat, and heavy calf muscles. Begin this exercise at a slow pace until you get the feel of the slide-and-slap movement. Then increase your tempo to a pace comfortable for you.

1 Sit on the floor, knees bent, feet flat, arms behind you supporting your body.

2 Point your right foot and slide (do not thump) your heel forward as you slap the back of the entire right leg on the floor.

3 Repeat with the left leg as you bring your right leg back to the original position.

RECOMMENDED REPETITIONS

For cellulite sufferers: 200 repetitions, each side
For heavy calves: 100–150 repetitions, each side
For cellulite prevention: 50 repetitions, each side

Leg Lifts

This exercise, along with Leg Circles and Bottom Shapers, is multifaceted: It shapes the leg, works the inner thigh area, promotes good circulation, and lifts and firms the derriere. So-called "secretary's spread" is not just some chauvinist's idea of a joke—it is an unfortunate reality for those with sedentary jobs, at any level. Because of lack of exercise, and poor posture, buttock muscles sag, cellulite develops, and the lower hips flatten and spread. Practicing these exercises faithfully will rid you of this unsightly condition forever.

1 Kneel on the floor, back straight, arms shoulder width apart and supporting you. Extend your right leg to the side and point your toe.

2 Inhale, and lift the entire leg up as high as you can. You will feel a stretch all along the leg, your inner thigh, and in the derriere.

3 Exhale, and lower your leg until it is 2 inches from the floor.

4 Without touching the floor, raise the leg 9 more times.

5 Repeat on the left side. Rest briefly. This is 1 set.

RECOMMENDED REPETITIONS

For sedentary spread: 3 sets of 10 repetitions, each side
For moderate firming: 2 sets of 10 repetitions, each side
For preventive maintenance: 1 set of 10 repetitions, each side

Leg Circles

1 Kneel on the floor, back straight, arms shoulder width apart and supporting you. Extend the right leg out to the side, knee straight, toe pointed.

2 Raise the right leg 6 inches from the floor and with your foot make as wide a circle as possible.

3 Make 10 circles before returning to the starting position.

4 Repeat on the left side. Rest briefly. This is 1 set.

RECOMMENDED REPETITIONS

For sedentary spread: 3 sets of 10 repetitions, each side
For moderate firming: 2 sets of 10 repetitions, each side
For preventive maintenance: 1 set of 10 repetitions, each side

Bottom Shapers

1 Kneel on the floor, back straight, arms shoulder width apart and supporting you. Extend the left leg out to the side, knee straight, toe pointed.

2 Bend the knee and bring it up until your thigh is parallel to the floor. (Yes, you will feel a profound stretch.)

Exercise as seen from above.

3 Keeping your torso straight, extend the leg straight out to the side, and then bring it back as you try to touch your derriere with your foot.

4 Without lowering the leg, move it out and back 9 more times before returning to the starting position.

5 Repeat the entire sequence on the right side. Rest briefly. This is 1 set.

RECOMMENDED REPETITIONS

For sedentary spread: 3 sets of 10 repetitions, each side

For moderate firming: 2 sets of 10 repetitions, each side

For preventive maintenance: 1 set of 10 repetitions, each side

The Double Kickback

Here is an exercise that should be done faithfully if your derriere is really out of shape, and if you are sedentary most of the time. It works directly on the muscles of the buttocks, lifting and rounding them. It also stretches the spine, promoting youthful flexibility.

1   Kneel on the floor, back straight, arms shoulder width apart, and supporting you.

2   Inhale, and bring your right knee forward until it touches your chin. At the same time, lower your head toward your chest.

3   Exhale, and extend your right leg straight back and up, kicking as high as possible. At the same time, stretch your chin toward the ceiling.

4 Keeping your leg straight, lower it until it is 2 inches from the floor, then kick up again, and inhale.

5 Bring the leg back to its starting position as you exhale.

6 Repeat 9 more times on the right side, then do 10 times on the left side. Rest briefly. This is 1 set.

RECOMMENDED REPETITIONS

For very flabby derriere or for cellulite: 3 sets of 10 repetitions, each side

For moderately out-of-shape derriere: 2 sets of 10 repetitions, each side

For preventive maintenance and flexibility: 1 set of 10 repetitions, each side

The Side Lunge

The inner thigh presents a real problem for heavy and thin women alike. It gets very little attention until it is almost too late. Have you ever noticed that dancers never suffer from flabby inner thighs, no matter what their ages? It's because they keep their muscles working and flexible. Here is an exercise that will work *your* inner thigh vigorously.

1   Stand with your legs straight, hands on hips, and feet 3½ to 4 feet apart (more if you are very tall).

2   Turn your upper body and your right foot to the right side, at an angle of 90 degrees to your left foot.

3   Keeping your back and left leg straight, bend your right knee as deeply as you possibly can, and inhale, letting your back foot slide to its fullest extension. Work toward getting your lunging thigh parallel to the floor. (But this is *not* for beginners.)

4   Exhale as you *almost* straighten your right leg. Lunge again 9 times more before returning to your starting position.

5   Repeat exercise on your left side. Rest briefly. This is 1 set.

RECOMMENDED REPETITIONS

For very flabby inner thighs: 3–4 sets of 10 repetitions, each side

For slightly flabby inner thighs: 2 sets of 10 repetitions, each side

To maintain muscle tone, and for prevention: 1 set of 10 repetitions, each side

Squats

Most women over twenty-one, and especially over the age of thirty-five, do not exercise properly to maintain shapely thighs. If you don't use it, you lose it! (Underexercised thigh muscles undergo rapid muscle deterioration at around age thirty-five.) This exercise can't be beat for firming the frontal thigh area.

1 Stand tall, with feet slightly wider than shoulder width apart (more if you are very tall), arms in front of you. For more muscle definition, hold a 3-pound weight in each hand.

2 Keeping your back straight, bend deeply into a squatting position, inhaling. Hold momentarily.

3 Exhale, and return *almost* to your starting position, keeping your knees flexed. Bend 9 times more in succession before returning to your starting position. Rest briefly. This is 1 set.

RECOMMENDED REPETITIONS

For underdeveloped frontal thigh muscles:
2–3 sets of 10 repetitions, with weights

For firming thigh muscles: 1 set, with weights

For maintaining shapely thigh muscles and for cellulite prevention: 1 set, without weights

The Waist Bend

If you have been following your diet plan, I'm sure that you can see and feel a very definite reduction in the waist and abdominal region. Preservatives, sugar, and salt really wage war on the midsection. To further aid you in whittling your waistline, the Waist Bend and the Waist Twist are quick and effective. They are both simple and have been around a long time. If they have not been effective for you in the past, it is because you were not performing them correctly or because the repetitions were not high enough. Pay close attention to detail, and you will see and feel the difference.

1   Stand with your feet shoulder width apart, toes pointed straight ahead, knees flexed, and hands on hips.

2   Inhale, and bend to the left as far as possible, keeping both feet flat on the floor and the right shoulder back.

3   Exhale and return to your original position.

4   Repeat on the right side.

RECOMMENDED REPETITIONS

For thick waist: 100 repetitions, each side

For waist 2–3 inches out of proportion: 50–75 repetitions, each side

For preventive maintenance: 25–50 repetitions, each side

The Waist Twist

This exercise will remove excess flab from the diaphragm area as well as the waistline. It should *not* be practiced by anyone who has a bad back, as the back stretch puts pressure on this area.

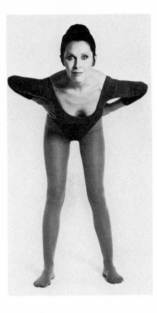

1   Stand tall, hands on hips, shoulders back, feet shoulder width apart with toes pointed straight ahead, knees flexed.

2   Inhale deeply.

3   Exhale, and lean straight forward from the waist. Point your chin up and stretch your upper body forward.

4   Inhale, as you slowly rotate your body to the right side, s-t-r-e-t-c-h-i-n-g the upper body as far to the side as possible. Exhale as you rotate to the back, leaning as far back as possible, and then inhale as you rotate your upper body slowly to the left side, keeping the upper body stretched.

5   Exhale as you return slowly to the front.

RECOMMENDED REPETITIONS

For heavy waist and diaphragm: 75 rotations

For waistline 2–3 inches too large: 50 rotations

For preventive maintenance: 25 rotations

The Bench Sit-up

For many years I have studied abdominal exercises with the purpose of finding the ones that work most quickly and effectively. For a long time it appeared that sit-ups and leg lifts were the best course, although results were not always as speedy as desired. Then one day I began experimenting with my husband's body-building exercises and found the effects on my students' tummies absolutely astounding. Now, both the Bench Sit-up and the Jackknife are important parts of the Body Sculpting regimen. Execute them very slowly and deliberately at first, then establish a rhythm and your breathing will become automatic.

1 Lie on your back in front of a heavy, stationary piece of furniture (such as a bed or sofa), feet flat on the floor and knees bent. Reach behind you and grasp a leg of the furniture with both hands.

2 Inhale, stretch your legs out at an angle of about 20 degrees from the floor, and point your toes.

3 Exhale, and try to touch your knees to your chest lifting your buttocks off the floor.

4 Inhale, and straighten your back as you thrust your legs out in front of you again.

5 Exhale as you return to your original position.

RECOMMENDED REPETITIONS

For very stretched abdomens: 20–30 repetitions
Following pregnancy: 10 repetitions, working up to 30
Moderately flabby: 15 repetitions
For preventive maintenance: 10 repetitions

The Jackknife

1   Sit on the floor with your knees bent and your feet as close as possible to your buttocks, your arms parallel to the floor at shoulder level, palms down.

2   Inhale, and lean as far back as possible, extending your legs straight out (the body forms a wide V). Hold your breath momentarily as you balance in this position.

3 Exhale, and pull your knees back to your chest.

4 Repeat 9 more times before resting briefly.

RECOMMENDED REPETITIONS

Very stretched or protruding abdomen: 20–30 repetitions

Following pregnancy: 10 repetitions, working up to 30

Moderately flabby: 20 repetitions

For preventive maintenance: 10 repetitions

FOR THE BUST

Flys

Despite controversy on the subject, I adamantly maintain that you *can* improve the shape and tone of your bustline considerably if you are willing to work at it. All you need is yourself and two weights of approximately 3 pounds each (dumbbells can be purchased in any sporting goods store, or use 3-pound juice cans or bricks instead). All of the bust exercises that follow are multifaceted: They work not only the chest and shoulders, but also the upper arm, particularly the triceps, which has a definite tendency to sag after thirty.

1 Lie on the floor with your knees bent, feet flat. Grasp a 3-pound weight in each hand and bring your arms straight up toward the ceiling, palms turned inward, weights touching each other. Do not lock your elbows.

2 Inhale as you lower the weights slowly to your sides and parallel to the bench, palms up.

3 Exhale as you bring the weights back to your starting position. Do 10 times. Rest briefly. This is 1 set.

RECOMMENDED REPETITIONS

For small bust, to increase: 3 sets of 10 repetitions, every other day
For average bust, to firm: 2 sets of 10 repetitions, every other day
For large bust: Do not perform this exercise

The Bench Press

For even better results, this exercise can be performed when lying on a bench (such as a piano bench, picnic bench, or weight-lifting bench if you have one).

1 Lie on the floor, knees bent, feet flat, back elevated off the floor (use a hard pillow). Grasp a 3-pound weight in each hand and bring the arms straight up toward the ceiling, palms facing forward. You should be able to see the backs of your hands.

2 Inhale as you bend your elbows and lower the weights slowly to your sides.

3 Exhale as you raise the weights again toward the ceiling. Do 10 times. Rest briefly. This is 1 set.

RECOMMENDED REPETITIONS

For small bust, to increase: 3 sets of 10 repetitions, every other day

For average bust, to firm: 2 sets of 10 repetitions, every other day

For large bust, to firm: 1 set of 10 repetitions, every other day

FOR THE BUST

The Pullover

1   Lie on the floor, knees bent, feet flat on the floor. Grasp a 3-pound weight in each hand and raise your arms toward the ceiling, palms facing forward.

2   Inhale as you lower the weights slowly behind your head. (Lock your elbows and keep your arms about 26 inches apart, until you touch the floor behind you.)

3   Exhale slowly and bring the weights back to starting position. Do 10 times. Rest briefly. This is 1 set.

RECOMMENDED REPETITIONS

For small bust, to increase: 3 sets of 10 repetitions, every other day

For average bust, to firm: 3 sets of 10 repetitions, every other day

For large bust, to firm and lift: 3 sets of 10 repetitions, every other day

For preventive maintenance: 2 sets of 10 repetitions, every other day

Arm Circles

This exercise is particularly good for firming flabby upper arms as well.

1 Stand with arms straight out to the side at shoulder level.

2 Make small circles with both arms, then bigger circles, then giant circles.

3 Continue circling until the upper arm and chest areas become warm, and the arms become tired.

RECOMMENDED REPITITIONS

For small bust, to increase: 15–25 revolutions, every other day

For average bust, to firm: 10–20 revolutions, every other day

For large bust, to firm: 15 revolutions, every other day

For preventive maintenance: 10 revolutions, every other day

Massage for the Knee and Ankle

The knees and ankles, which tend to retain fluid easily in the over-thirty woman, are two areas that respond more quickly to diet and massage than to exercise. I have seen women lose up to 2 inches from the knee in a week, and up to ½ inch from the ankle, when my diet and supplement program is followed faithfully. To further aid in the reduction of these areas, a do-it-yourself massage is extremely beneficial.

How to Massage

1 Sit on the floor with your legs extended in front of you. Relax your muscles.

2 Knead and pinch the tissue around your knee, down your calf, and around your ankle. Use a light oil so that you do not pull your skin or cause friction, but don't be tentative. Use strong, steady pressure to increase your circulation in these areas. If you have heavy knees or ankles or suffer from cellulite, massage daily. Others should massage whenever there is a tendency to retain fluids.

Some Exercise Tips

When it comes to the performance of an exercise, I'm a teacher who demands perfection. There is no reason to exercise at all if you do not perform the exercises correctly. Time and time again at health spas I have seen women halfheartedly performing their exercises, breathing incorrectly, and bitterly complaining that they see no results. When you exercise, monitor yourself in front of a full-length mirror, breathe correctly, and perform each motion separately and correctly. My directions are very specific, and I want you to be very specific with yourself!

Correct breathing can improve the results of your workout by as much as 50 percent. Many people breathe shallowly, or hold their breath when exercising. This inhibits circulation and holds tension in the muscles. Oxygen is needed for both the reduction and building of body parts.

Here are a few more tips:

- *Never* exercise immediately after eating. Wait at least two hours. This gives your body time to begin the process of digestion.

- If possible, exercise before breakfast. You will feel marvelously awake and alive all day, and you will remove all the stress and kinks that have accumulated during sleep. Morning exercise will benefit your complexion all day—your skin will become rosier and more glowing. Exercise acts as an appetite depressant, too—an all-day boon for those of you who are currently restricting your food intake. Best of all, when you exercise first thing in the morning, you won't have to worry about your exercises the rest of the day!

- Do not take a sauna or a hot bath immediately after exercising. You will relax your muscles too quickly, and thus lose some of the results of your workout.

- Do not drink hot or cold liquids when exercising. This can cause cramping. A sip of room-temperature water is allowed.

- Do not hurry through your routine. Remember, the time you spend will pay off in a healthy, youthful, and beautiful body.

- After completing any lying-down exercise, do not get up too quickly. Breathe deeply a few times, and come up to a sitting or standing position slowly, to prevent dizziness.

- Take exercise breaks instead of coffee breaks during the day. Go into the ladies' lounge at work and practice your wall bends and stretches. You'll feel rejuvenated and refreshed when you return to your desk. Take your yeast and juice break after your exercise break. (Try it—it will soon become a habit.)

- When possible, exercise out-of-doors. Clear a corner of your yard or patio for your routine. The fresh air will promote better circulation, and exercising in a natural setting will increase your enjoyment.

Week Three

Natural Care for Healthy Skin

FOR the past two weeks, you have been hard at work. I know there have been times that have been difficult, as you struggled with withdrawal symptoms from addictive foods and experienced aches and pains from your strenuous Body Sculpting regimen. But it has been worth it, hasn't it? You can now see the beginnings of a radiant new you as you confront your mirror honestly. Your figure is definitely curvier, your skin is much improved, your eyes are shining, and your cheeks are rosy. Best of all, you feel terrific! Your energy level is rising daily, and you're sleeping more soundly. You probably have had some compliments, too, as friends, relatives, and co-workers observe your transformation.

At this point, your diet is becoming a habit, as is your exercise program. You are losing your taste for the debilitated foods you once enjoyed, and a few weeks from now you won't even remember them fondly. Because of your increased energy level and visible figure improvement, Body Sculpting is a vital part of your day.

For the third week of your program, I have planned a pleasant surprise. This will be a week of pampering yourself a little—you've earned it! Our focus now will be on your skin, and on the development of a quick, easy, effective, and pleasurable routine that will keep it glowing and youthful-looking for the rest of your life.

Good Skin Begins from Within

From time immemorial, beautiful skin has been considered one of a woman's most important physical assets. In addition, it is a glowing affirmation of health, as the skin is one of the first indicators of a state of well-being. Most of us were born with flawless skin, but, alas, as we progress from childhood to adolescence, dietary indiscretions, the production of hormones, and experimentation with cosmetics often combine to produce a woefully far-from-perfect skin. After the age of thirty little signs of aging begin to appear, and many women throw up their hands in either resignation or despair. Although some signs of aging are inevitable, I believe that with proper care the skin, which is remarkably resilient, can either retain or regain a youthful appearance. Attention to nutrition and to proper circulation is absolutely mandatory if you want a glowing complexion. Pollution in diet (and this includes alcohol and cigarettes) can muddy the skin, create under-eye circles, and dull the eyes very quickly. Particularly after thirty the effects of a late night out on the town are instantly visible the next day. We must determine to be kind to ourselves, and not subject our skin to the ravages of late nights, or too much booze, or foods debilitating to our health.

As a person who really suffered from frequent and embarrassing skin eruptions from adolescence until my conversion to a more healthful way of life, I can truly empathize with any readers suffering with skin problems. Because of my personal problem, I have thoroughly researched and studied literally hundreds of skin care and cosmetic programs. I have tested and retested products and methods on myself and my students, and I have always asked any woman with flawless skin for her secret. For the past few years I have been working with what I now consider to be a superior skin care method, which I would like to pass on to you. Caring for your skin requires very

97

little time or expense. What it does require is the self-discipline of daily exercise and good nutrition and a simple routine, followed faithfully every day.

Determine Your Skin Type

Observe your freshly cleansed face closely in the mirror. Is it *oily?* Oily skin often manifests itself around adolescence with a tendency to blemishes, large pores, and a coarse texture. Makeup melts into the skin soon after application, and blackheads, whiteheads, excessive perspiration, and even acne may create additional problems. This type of skin can be found in any age group—although far more common among women in their teens and twenties, excessive oiliness sometimes plagues women well into their fifties. The elimination of sugar, preservatives, and fried foods on this plan, and the addition of brewer's yeast, will aid in diminishing oily skin outbreaks. The good news about oily skin is that with proper care it can remain dewy and youthful in appearance for a long time.

Perhaps your skin is *dry*. Many women experience the beginnings of dryness around the age of twenty-three, although dry skin can and does manifest itself as early as the late teens. As the skin dries, many moisturizers become ineffective, the skin chafes and flakes easily, and fine lines become etched on the surface. These lines usually appear first around the outer corner of the eyes, either side of the nose and mouth, then on the forehead and between the eyebrows. The skin often appears to be thin, and feels tight after cleansing. Fortunately, there is help for dry skin, and when carefully tended to, this skin type can become normal.

Lucky the woman who possesses *normal* skin! In this day and age, she is uncommon indeed. Normal skin is smooth and even in color. Several hours after cleansing, it remains glowing, never greasy. Lines are minimal, even in the mature woman, and there is no sagging. The pores are small, and there are no under-eye circles.

Sensitive skin is another skin type that deserves our attention. It can be accompanied by either oiliness or dryness, and seems to be increasing as our lifestyles become more complex. Sensitive skin is quick to respond to stress, spicy food, alcohol, tobacco, caffeine, sugar, cosmetics, and drugs. Under-eye circles are not uncommon. Blotchiness or under-the-surface blemishes may appear quickly. Tiny red blood vessels often appear on the nose and cheeks following exposure to the sun, or after ingestion of drugs, spicy foods, or alcohol. All these conditions, though distressing, are both preventable and treatable.

As you determine your skin type, bear in mind that many people have *combination* skin—for example, you may have sensitive skin with oiliness around the nose and chin. The cheeks and forehead may be dry or normal. Treat the oily areas as you would oily skin, and the other areas accordingly.

A Simple Cleansing Program That Works

The first step in any skin care program is proper cleansing. This should be done without fail twice daily, morning and night. The first cleansing of the day is most important, for beauty sleep is just what the phrase implies. During the night, when your body is resting, the skin is hard at work throwing off cellular debris. This is why your skin often looks dull or dingy when you awake. You must get rid of all this waste material before moisturizing or making up.

Never, never go to bed with your makeup on—if you do, your skin will absorb oil and grease as you sleep, and you may develop a real problem with blemishes, blackheads, and whiteheads. Clogged pores will prevent the cellular wastes normally thrown off during sleep from reaching the skin's surface, and serious flare-ups may result.

Whenever you apply cleansing or cosmetic products to the face, use gentle upward and outward movements of your fingers. The delicate skin of the face is constantly exposed to the assaults of weather and the forces of gravity. To counteract this, reverse the force of gravity with your motions. As you cleanse the throat area (always remember that your neck is part of your face), stroke upward in a diagonal line from left to right, and then from right to left. Do not use your thumbs. Then apply your cleanser under the chin, slapping the area with the back of your hand to promote good circulation and firmness. Stroke upward from the chin to the cheeks, from the cheeks to the temples, and from the temples to the hairline. Circle the mouth and the eyes gently with your fingers. (These areas are very delicate and contain few oil glands.) Stroke up the sides of your nose and down the bridge (the only downward stroke on the entire face). Apply all cosmetics, except for foundation and powder, with these strokes. They are a beauty treatment in themselves.

Now, on to cleansing products. Remember I told you that I must have tried every product imaginable in my quest for a good skin? And that I have queried beautiful-skinned people as to their secrets? Well, time after time, to my surprise, I found that the answers to my questions were amazingly simple and inexpensive routines, as well as being almost unanimously the same. All these women credited their beautiful skin to the use of natural products. All the products they used for basic skin care contained protein. Protein is vital to skin beauty. Collagen (the fibrous connective tissue collagen is the protein substance that keeps skin young, firm, and moist), elastin (a "youth" substance produced by the body, which begins to diminish around the age of twenty-five), and moisture are

The proper way to apply cleansing and cosmetic products.

three substances that nourish the skin. Since the skin is absorbent, it makes sense to apply a high-grade protein to it. For women with normal and dry skin tendencies I have found simple nonfat dry milk powder to be extremely effective as a cleanser; for those with oily or sensitive skin tendencies yogurt works equally well. My own skin tends to be extremely oily, but two weeks after I began to use yogurt on my face the oiliness was well under control. Naturally, I told my students of my discovery, and the results they experienced were equally amazing. As it turns out, my "secret" has been used by legendary beauties for thousands of years. Cleopatra bathed in milk, and the Empress Josephine swore by it also, to name just two milk enthusiasts. The list is endless, but the method is tried, true, and inexpensive.

101

FOR NORMAL TO DRY SKIN

Wet your hands. Pour a small amount of nonfat dry milk powder on the palm and dip your fingers in it. The milk will stick to your fingers like a coating. Apply the milk to the face and neck, using the cleansing strokes described earlier and making sure to cover all areas. Let the milk soak into your skin for 60 seconds, then splash with water hot as your hands can stand, 30 times. Finish with a splash of cold water. Pat—never rub—your face with a clean towel.

FOR OILY SKIN

Apply a paste of plain yogurt to your face with the cleansing strokes, rinse 30 times, apply the yogurt again, and let it remain on your skin for 60 seconds. Rinse again 30 times with hot water, and follow with a cool-water splash to close the pores. Pat your face dry with a clean towel. If you have very enlarged pores, apply an ice cube wrapped in a washcloth to the offending areas. Your pores will appear greatly diminished, and the skin will glow with improved circulation.

MILK IN THE BATH

Not only is milk protein beautifying to facial skin, it is beneficial when used in the bath, too. (Think of all those expensive cosmetics labeled "milk bath," which contain all sorts of chemicals and additives and only a fraction of milk!) From now on, make your own more potent milk bath inexpensively. Pour ½ cup nonfat dry milk into the tub, directly under the tap. Add a few drops of your favorite fragrance. The milk will bubble like a commercial bubble bath, with absolutely no milky smell. Soak in a warm tub for a few minutes, wash, pat dry, and enjoy the feel of your satiny skin!

If your body skin is very dry, in addition to the milk, put ½ cup of uncooked oatmeal tied in an old stocking in the tub with you. You will be amazed at how quickly your skin will respond to this natural and inexpensive softening agent.

CONSUMER BEWARE

It is a psychological fact that all human beings are attracted to beauty. We women in particular fall prey as consumers to expensive cosmetic gimmicks because of beautiful packaging. Good skin care does not have to be expensive. Buy the prettiest covered container you can find for the nonfat dry milk or yogurt you use as a cleanser. You'll enjoy using it every time, and your container will truly be an original. Keep perishable items in the refrigerator, and keep all containers scrupulously clean. Remember, these products contain no preservatives, so care must be taken to prevent bacteria from forming. Never let anyone else use your cosmetics.

The Next Step: Toning

After your cleansing routine is completed, it's time to apply a freshener, which helps to balance the skin. An excellent freshener for dry, sensitive, and normal skin is chamomile tea. For many years Hungarian women have prided themselves on their beautiful skin, and one of their little-known secrets is the use of chamomile, which grows abundantly in their country. Make a full-strength tea solution with chamomile teabags (available in most supermarkets and health food stores), pour it into a sterile jar, cover tightly, and refrigerate. After cleansing, saturate a cosmetic sponge or piece of cotton with the tea and apply it to your face. The chamomile forms a light, protective cover on the skin, and helps to normalize it.

If your skin is oily, a vinegar-and-water freshener will help control the shine. In a sterile jar, combine 1 part apple cider vinegar with 7 parts spring water, cover tightly, and refrigerate. After cleansing, dip a piece of cotton or cosmetic sponge into the solution and pat it onto your face. You will be pleasantly surprised to find that it significantly decreases the oil flow.

Moisturizing

The pure spring water you have been drinking on this program has been moisturizing your skin from within by rehydrating and plumping up the skin cells. Now, following the application of freshener, it is important to use an external moisturizer. Every skin, even an oily one, will benefit from its use. Remember, oil is not the same as moisture. If you use a light foundation, I recommend a commercial moisturizer, which is specifically formulated as an under-makeup base. However, be extremely selective in your choice of moisturizer. As with foods, read labels. There is a cosmetic labeling law now in effect—use it. Skin problems can be compounded by the indiscriminate use of inferior products. Some good commercial moisturizers my students and I have found beneficial are Mill Creek, Lancôme, Payot, and Clinique. Dilute the moisturizer with spring water before applying it. Not only will this save you money but your skin will absorb the moisturizer better and your makeup will go on more smoothly.

Moisturizing the body after a bath is as important as moisturizing the face. If you neglect your body skin, dryness and annoying flaking will result. A good body moisturizer is Nivea skin oil, an old formula that is recommended by just about every masseuse I have ever met. Another good, inexpensive skin product is Vaseline Intensive Care Lotion. And for those of you who live in a cold climate, a good practice is to use Vaseline as a body moisturizer once a week. In fall, the skin starts to "thin down" with every drop in temperature. By the time winter rolls around, everyone's skin is at its thinnest, and all of us need extra protection against the dryness that results. To accomplish this, take a small amount of Vaseline (too much is unpleasant) and massage it well into your body skin—it will not be greasy. Leave it on overnight, and wake up with beautifully soft, smooth skin. This is another skin secret that has been used for many years by legendary beauties.

MOISTURIZING FROM WITHIN

If your skin is *excessively* dry and chafed—a condition that seems particularly to plague women going through menopause—you might try a nutritional remedy that is age-old and still very effective: cod liver oil. Every day before breakfast take 2 tablespoons of cod liver oil mixed with 4 ounces of fresh orange juice or milk, and watch the improvement in your skin as well as in the texture and sheen of your hair. Dale Alexander, a nutritional consultant from California who wrote the book *Dry Skin and Cod Liver Oil*, says that you will see definite results within six months, but my students have experienced much speedier results.

Exfoliation

A practice that must be incorporated into any optimum skin care routine is exfoliation. Our skin cells constantly renew themselves—one reason why we can improve our skin so dramatically. As new cells form, old ones dry up, and if they are not removed frequently, they form a dull film on the skin that prevents it from showing its true beauty. In addition, dead cells can clog pores and inhibit circulation. To remove these dead cells, which form on all skin types, it is necessary to use a mild abrasive that will slough them off the surface of the skin and encourage the growth of fresh, new cells. This abrasive material should always be used gently, with upward, circular strokes, as too much pressure is detrimental to any type of skin.

A good exfoliating agent for oily skin is the Buf-Puf, a synthetic sponge formulated by a dermatalogist and available in any drugstore. It can be used with your yogurt cleanser. If you feel that this treatment is too abrasive for you, try one of the all-natural honey-and-almond scrubs found in any health food store, or make your own scrub of almonds crushed in the blender and mixed with a little raw honey. (The homemade mixture is a little sticky and takes longer to use.) For sensitive and dry skin, a gentle and effective product is Aapri Scrub— made of polished apricot kernels, it is a natural formula that has been in use for many years. It is found in most health food stores and elsewhere.

One of the best friends your body skin will ever have is a loofah sponge, which you can buy in a pharmacy or department or specialty store for about three dollars. It is a natural vegetable sponge, which has been used by European women for hundreds of years to "polish" the skin and to help prevent cellulite deposits. It greatly aids circulation, too. Many "imitation loofahs," which claim to "magically dissolve cellulite," abound on the market presently, and it constantly amazes me that manufacturers continue to command as much as twenty-five dollars for one of these plastic gimmicks, which work no better than (and often not as well as) the inexpensive loofah. The secret of the loofah is that *it must be used daily*. French women use it dry, but for most of us it is more comfortable used in conjunction with the bath. Stroke the loofah upward on your body, always going in the direction of the heart. Use a firm, constant pressure as you cover the entire surface of your arms and legs; use a rotating, circular motion on your buttocks, abdomen, upper chest, and shoulders. Soon you will note that your circulation is much better, and that your skin is more resilient, more even in tone, and more satiny in texture. If you suffer from cellulite, you will find that as you use your loofah in combination with the diet and exercise program, the condition will diminish quickly. The loofah is a nice preventive skin care method to teach a daughter at an early age.

Night Creams

The next step in your skin care routine is the addition of a night and body cream that is truly an amazing discovery. If you are over thirty, no doubt the first signs of aging have already begun to appear on your skin. Tiny lines, wrinkles, and stretch marks may disturb you. If you have a tendency to gain and lose weight quickly, the skin is no doubt stretched. (The best remedy for this, obviously, is to stabilize your weight once and for all.) Your skin may not be as firm as it once was, and you may have noticed the beginnings of bags or pouches under the eyes. While all of these problems are certainly disheartening, they can be reversed to some extent with elastin, a substance produced naturally by the skin that begins to diminish around the age of twenty-five. French dermatologists have been working with it for years and report that elastin cream is the most potent discovery to date in the fight against the aging skin. Here are some of the findings of the French doctors whose patients used elastin cream on a regular basis:

- decrease in the appearance of stretch marks
- prevention of stretch marks during pregnancy
- firming of neck, inner thighs, breasts, and upper arms, as well as other body areas
- lessening of wrinkles around the eyes, upper lip, and corners of the lips
- disappearance of under-eye pouches

107

I have been using elastin on the inner thigh area, where I had some stretch marks resulting from pregnancy, and on little lines around the eyes, which I foolishly acquired during a winter vacation in Guadeloupe. Both conditions have improved amazingly.

For women over forty or for younger women with double chins, I highly recommend the use of elastin in conjunction with a neck exercise. I have seen some truly remarkable examples of mature women "turning back the clock" when this exercise is performed faithfully every night.

The Neck Stretch

1 Lie on your back on the bed. Inhale and exhale deeply a few times.

2 Hang your shoulders over the edge of the bed, and slowly let your head drop backward as you inhale. Go as far back as you can comfortably stretch and hold your breath as you hold the stretch.

3 Exhale as you s-l-o-w-l-y begin to raise your head and try to touch your chin to your chest.

4 Do 10 times.

Elastin is best applied at night. The skin must be thoroughly cleansed so that the cream can penetrate deeply. Elastin is then massaged into the areas that need the treatment. (I suggest that the entire face and body be treated.) The doctors suggest that elastin in the pure form be used every day for a month, then every other day, forever, on the face. Body cream, which is less expensive, and which contains less elastin, should be used continuously on the body skin. I tried the pure cream on the inner thigh area, and found it to be more effective. The best buys that I have found to date are Elastin and Elastin Body Lotion, produced by the Mill Creek Cosmetic Company. These products can be purchased in health food stores and in some large department stores.

Another nighttime moisturizer that is inexpensive and nonallergenic is very lightly applied petroleum jelly, or Vaseline. Have you ever noticed that the main ingredient in many creams and lotions is petrolatum? Why pay the high prices demanded by cosmetic companies, and expose yourself to the possibility of an allergy as well, when a very light application of Vaseline will do the job as effectively! Applied very lightly, it will penetrate the skin quickly and leave no greasy residue.

A Weekly Facial

Here is an easy, inexpensive facial routine that will take approximately an hour of your time once a week. It will help you maintain a soft, smooth complexion and will promote good circulation.

Put a large pot of water on the stove to boil. When it comes to a high boil, add 3 tablespoons of Swiss Kriss, a mixture of herbs available in health food stores. Boil the herbs for 3 minutes and then remove the pot from the stove. Set it on a sturdy table. Put your thoroughly clean face close to the pot and make a tent with a towel, covering your head and the sides of the pot with it. The vapor from the water and herbs will deep-cleanse your face, removing pollution and impurities. Let the steam penetrate for 5 to 10 minutes. Then thoroughly cleanse your face again. You are now ready for a natural mask.

If you have oily or sensitive skin, the following mask works well: Mix equal parts of wheat germ and yogurt. Apply this to the skin, and leave it on until the mixture dries. Rinse with hot water, splashing your face 30 times. Then apply your usual moisturizer.

If you have dry skin, mix a small amount of uncooked oatmeal with the yolk of an egg, apply it to your face, and let it dry. The egg is protein, which will nourish your skin, and the oatmeal has skin-softening properties. The white of an egg can be used as a mask to diminish tiny lines and wrinkles, and can be left on all night, if desired. Remove both these masks with 30 splashes of hot water.

A very good mask for blemished skin is a mixture of brewer's yeast and a small amount of water (just enough so that the yeast becomes doughy). Apply this mixture to the affected areas and leave it on for at least 30 minutes, or overnight if you wish. The yeast really helps to dry up blemishes.

While your mask is drying, do not talk if at all possible. If the pores of your face are larger than you like, take damp towels that were put in the freezer for 10 minutes and apply to your face while the mask dries. To increase the efficacy of the mask further, lie on a slant board while it dries.

THE SLANT BOARD

The slant board is, as far as I am concerned, one of the most important beauty aids you can use. It is a board that is raised 18 inches off the floor at one end so that the head rests at the lower end and the feet are at the raised end. Blood flows from the feet and legs into the trunk and face, the force of gravity is reversed, and muscles and organs rest and get a "lift." The increased flow of circulation to the face and trunk has a rejuvenating effect on the entire body. Many famous beauties swear by the use of the slant board. Some even claim that regular use from a young age will negate the need for a face lift in later life! Not only is the slant board a beauty boon—you will get a definite psychological lift out of relaxing a few minutes daily on it. After using it, you will experience a resurgence of energy throughout your entire body. One note of caution: Do not use the slant board when you are menstruating, or if you suffer from high blood pressure.

If you cannot find a slant board in your sporting goods store, you may have to ask that one be special-ordered for you, but it will be well worth it. If space is a problem, do what my students do—hang the slant board (which can be covered in a pretty fabric) on a large hook on the back of your bedroom door, where it will be easily accessible yet unobtrusive.

A Facial Exercise to Keep You Youthful

Many reputable authorities in the beauty and health field know that facial exercise can be helpful in maintaining a youthful appearance. Dr. Willibald Nagler of the New York Hospital–Cornell Medical Center reported in *Vogue* recently: "Facial exercise, like all exercise, can strengthen and tone muscles, especially around your neck and mouth—and can help to prevent muscles from sagging and showing early signs of age." He emphasized that, in order to be effective, the exercise must be done daily.

As a beauty consultant, I can emphatically support facial exercise as a preventive measure against early aging—and furthermore, I have seen amazing rejuvenating effects upon mature faces from the faithful practice of facial exercise. The face contains fifty-five muscles, and, like any other muscles, they must be utilized or they atrophy.

I have found one exercise in particular to be highly effective in working the entire face; more specifically, it helps to prevent lines from forming around the eyes and mouth. It is very funny-looking, so it is best done in solitude, if you do not want a laughing audience.

It may take a few repetitions to get the hang of this exercise. When you are doing it correctly your entire face will feel warm from the increase in facial circulation. This exercise also re-

111

moves tension, which commonly builds in the face.

The Lion

1 Sit straight, close your eyes, and take three deep breaths.

2 On your fourth breath, inhale deeply and then exhale, expelling the air from your lungs with a loud "Ha!" At the same time, pop your eyes open as far as possible, open your mouth in a big, round O, and stick your tongue out and down toward your chin.

3 Hold the position for as long as you can (try not to laugh), then breathe deeply a few times and repeat the exercise once more. Do twice daily.

The Sun and Your Skin

As any dermatologist will tell you, too much sun is definitely detrimental to your skin. Indiscriminate sun worshipping can result in premature aging, irregular pigmentation, and, most serious, skin cancer.

I am not going to tell you that you may never go out in the sun—that would be impractical—but be aware that overexposure ages skin terribly. Never stay in the sun long enough to get a sunburn. The safest tan is achieved by sunning just enough so that the skin blushes slightly. And until your tolerance to the sun is built up, avoid the midday sun.

Because of the concern expressed by dermatologists, cosmetic companies have jumped on the bandwagon with groups of sunscreen products rated for their SPF—Sun Protection Factor. The higher the SPF number, the greater the protection from the sun. Thus, a lotion that is labeled SPF 6 will give you some protection from the sun's rays, while a lotion that is labeled SPF 16 will give you high protection and one labeled SPF 19 will virtually block the sun's rays. Take advantage of these products—select one which will protect your skin best, and use it before sun exposure and at least once per hour while you are in the sun.

If, unfortunately, you should somehow contract a sunburn, the best remedy I know of is the tea bath. Tea contains tannic acid, which will calm the skin. Draw a tepid bath, and to it add a whole pot of strong tea (or, lacking that, a cup of vinegar). Soak in the tub for at least a half hour, allowing the bath to soothe your skin. Pat yourself dry gently (no loofah today) and apply a Vitamin E cream or Vitamin A + D cream (containing allantoin, a healing agent) to the affected areas. For the rest of the season, avoid the midday sun entirely, as your now-sensitized skin will all too readily absorb the sun's damaging rays.

A little prevention is worth a pound of cure in the area of sunbathing, and although as a health enthusiast I know that fresh air and sunshine are beauty and health boosters, sunshine can also be a health and beauty boomerang when not approached with respect.

A Few Words About Hair and Nail Care

As I mentioned in the very beginning of this chapter, no doubt by now you have noticed an improvement in your skin due to your new diet. Well, look more closely—I'll bet your hair is getting shinier and thicker, and your nails are growing a little longer, too. Although hair and nails take longer to show dramatic improvement when the diet is altered, in the long run diet can produce such a gorgeous crop of hair or set of nails that it is sometimes visually startling.

It is common knowledge that nutrients such as brewer's yeast and cod liver oil are added to the diets of show animals to keep their fur lustrous; it is not-so-common knowledge that these foods can make human hair lustrous, too. So often we

113

look to shampoos or conditioners as the answer to overly dry or oily hair, when all that may be needed is a change in diet. If you suffer from dry, brittle hair, add the cod liver oil routine described earlier in this chapter to your morning regimen, and within six to eight weeks your hair will be improved. If you suffer from an oily scalp, religiously avoid fried foods and animal fats, and do not neglect to flush your system each day with 8 to 10 glasses of spring water. If an acne condition accompanies your oily scalp (acne is *not* just a teenage problem), I strongly advise you to consult with a good dermatologist trained in the latest preventive and curative methods. At the Orentreich Research Foundation in New York City, for example, doctors like Alan Epstein are doing miraculous work in individualized hormonal treatment of acne. Never forget that for hair, as well as for skin, beauty begins from within.

Strong hair and nails are heavily dependent on adequate amounts of protein in the diet, so make sure that you are getting optimum amounts of the highest-quality protein available. Hair and nails will respond negatively to stress and pressure, and adequate amounts of Vitamin B in the diet will help to assure their continued growth. (Some cases of hair loss have been traced directly to Vitamin B deficiency.)

The slant board is a beauty treatment for hair, too. Many cases of thinning hair and falling hair were reversed when proper circulation was restored to the head. The slant board is a delightful and effortless way to make sure that your scalp is receiving adequate blood and oxygen. While you are lying on it, massage your scalp gently in a rotating motion with the pads of your fingers. Begin at the base of the skull, working around and then inward until the entire head has been massaged.

There are some simple external procedures that can help to promote hair and nail beauty between salon visits. As with health, professional care is occasionally necessary, but the responsibility ultimately lies with the individual.

Cleansing the hair is vitally important; how frequently depends upon the type of hair. Oily hair may be shampooed every day, while normal to dry hair responds best to a shampoo every two to three days. A tip from professional hairdressers: Dilute your commercial shampoo by half with water. Full-strength shampoo leaves a heavy coating on hair, which may be mistaken for lankness, dullness, or excessive flaking or oiliness. Rinsing is extremely important—a film of soap left in the hair can dull even the most glorious mane. If your hair is oily, avoid shampoos labeled "balsam" or "protein"—these will leave your hair limp and sticky, and are preparations better suited for dry hair. Many shampoos have been improved by the addition of keratin, a protein substance that coats the hair shaft, adding body, luster, and fullness. Shampoo containing a jojoba oil aids in the control of dandruff and oiliness, and some enthusiastic hair professionals are even claiming that jojoba oil is responsible for stimulating new hair growth in formerly balding clients!

After your hair has been cleansed and rinsed thoroughly, follow up with a cold rinse of vinegar and water if your hair is oily, or chamomile and water if your hair is dry. Then gently towel-dry your hair and comb out the tangles with a wide-tooth comb—never brush your hair when it is wet, or it can break. If at all possible, let your hair dry naturally. If this is not possible, blow-dry it until damp, and then let it dry naturally. Most experts agree that excessive heat (and sun, too) is damaging to the hair, so avoid it as much as possible.

What about conditioners? Every hair professional of my acquaintance has stressed their importance in keeping the hair manageable and lustrous. There are basically two types of conditioners: instant conditioners and penetrating conditioners. Instant conditioners temporarily coat the hair shaft, helping the hair look and feel more luxurious. Penetrating conditioners actually improve the hair by penetrating the shaft, and are a good addition to any beauty regimen on at least a monthly basis. An easy instant conditioner is the addition of an egg whipped into the shampoo. A good penetrating conditioner is Jheri' Redding's Nutri-Pak, which must be left on the cleansed hair for a few minutes following its application. Another easy (but messy) once-a-month conditioner is the combination of warm vegetable oil and a whipped egg. Apply it to the entire head following your shampoo. Cover your head with Saran Wrap and then with a hot towel. Let the oil work on your hair for an hour, then shampoo well (you may need up to three applications of shampoo) and rinse thoroughly, ending with a cold-water rinse. When your hair dries, it will gleam.

Much has been written and discussed about the pros and cons of henna, a natural dye and conditioner. I believe that it is highly beneficial when used correctly by a competent professional. Henna can be damaging, both in quality of color and in overdrying, when it is an inferior grade of henna or has been applied incorrectly. Hennaing is a time-consuming and tedious process—the product must be left on the hair for some time if it is to be effective. Some hair professionals combine yogurt with henna for a more concentrated protein conditioner. I have seen some beautiful heads of hair resulting from the careful professional application of henna, and some strawlike, strangely colored thatches resulting from do-it-yourself jobs.

In the summer, protect your hair from the ravages of chlorinated pools, excess heat, and sun, just as you protect your skin. Sun dries and blisters hair, so wear a scarf or hat over your crowning glory when you are gardening or at the beach. If your hair gets saturated with water from a heavily chlorinated pool, wash it just as soon as possible. Chlorine can dry and dull hair quickly, and if your hair is bleached, it can turn green.

Some companies now make special products designed to coat the hair protectively while you are exposed to summer hazards. If your hair has a tendency toward brittleness or dryness, or is permed or processed, I would recommend one of these as a preventive measure.

Our hands are constantly in view, and graceful, well-manicured nails are a definite beauty asset. No one today expects a woman's nails to be the long, oval, exotically colored works of art that were considered beautiful thirty years ago. But shapely, healthy-looking nails are a sophisticated finishing touch to the look of healthy vitality that we wish to project. A few minutes per week can assure us of lovely hands. On the evening of the week designated for your facial steam, tend to your nails at the same time. Remove the polish with firm strokes from the cuticle outward to the tip of the nail. Then file your nails into a gently rounded shape, making sure they are a uniform length. File in one direction only, from the base of the nail to the tip—"sawing" back and forth with a file or emery board weakens the nail. Now apply a little vegetable oil to the cuticles, and immerse your hands in a small dish of soapy water while your face is steaming. After the steam, rinse your hands and gently push the cuticles away from the nails with an orange stick. Use the other end of the orange stick to gently loosen any dirt under the nails. Then, with a buffer (an old-fashioned manicure tool that can be purchased in most drugstores), buff your nails until the skin underneath glows pink. Following this, apply a clear polish and, if your nails are long enough, a colored polish in a fashionable tone.

A once-a-month pedicure is usually sufficient, unless the cuticles are unusually thick or the nails grow very rapidly.

If, on occasion, your hands or feet are very dry, or if they are overexposed to the sun or wind, massage a light coat of Vaseline into them before bedtime and then cover them with cotton gloves or socks, accordingly. Leave the coverings on over-

117

night—in the morning your skin and cuticles will be baby-soft and smooth.

You now have a program for your skin, hair, and nails that will really work for you. Be faithful about it, and in a little notebook record the many positive changes that you will see. This will provide continued motivation and help you to remember just how far you have progressed. A glowing skin, lovely hair, and healthy nails are easily acquired with just a little time and attention. The few minutes spent in daily care will result in a more youthful complexion and increased joy, pride, and confidence in yourself.

Week Four

Improving Posture and Body Alignment

YOU are at the beginning of the fourth week of your health and beauty program. You should be absolutely delighted with your new image. Compliments are coming your way daily as your real beauty and vitality continue to emerge. Your diet and exercise routines are easy now—you have no desire to cheat because the rewards are more than worth any effort you have had to expend. Your program of skin care is becoming routine now, too, and your face and body glow from the simple but effective care you have given them during the past week. As you continue to make your diet, exercises, and skin care program an everyday part of your life, you are eager to learn and to apply more of the principles of health and beauty that will make you even more vibrant. You are now ready to work on achieving perfect posture and correct body alignment.

Have you ever attended a really professional fashion show, or a dance performance by well-known artists? If you have, I am sure that you were thrilled by the beautiful movements of the models or dancers, and that, through watching them, you became a little more aware of the way *your* body moves. Long ago, when I first learned the art of visual poise, or correct body movement, I became aware that proper posture is one of the most important, as well as one of the most neglected, forms of physical culture. A beautiful body in motion gives the instant impression of charm, grace, and self-confidence; even more important, correct posture is necessary for an optimum state of health. When we are young—in our teens or in our early twenties—the effects of poor posture are not yet apparent. But as the thirtieth birthday approaches, postural mistakes "suddenly" crop up. Many people do not realize that, for example, a rounded tummy (which is the bane of many over-thirty women, fat or thin) or protruding thighs are the direct result of years of incorrect movement. The dowager's hump, a rounding of the shoulders that becomes permanent, appears gradually and then becomes a painful reminder of years of slumping. Sagging fannies, underdeveloped thigh muscles, large calves, and droopy breasts are often attributable to poor posture, as are varicose veins, which mar many a pretty leg.

Think back, for a moment, to our model or dancer. She may not really be classically beautiful, but her body is in good shape, her grooming is impeccable, she radiates good health, and her posture is superb. She gives the impression of great beauty and youthfulness. Think, on the other hand, of a seated woman who at first glance appears striking. Her hair is coiffed beautifully, she is fashionably dressed and made up—and then she stands up. As she moves across the room, her head goes down self-consciously, her stomach protrudes ever so slightly, and her shoulders come forward—just a little. Alas, the beautiful impression is marred, and neglect of just this one aspect of beauty and health creates a picture far short of what was obviously intended.

Correct body movement and posture are indispensable to true beauty and health. Think of the joy you feel when you see a beautiful racehorse in motion—the body moves effortlessly, flowing from one movement into another. So should we move—without stiffness, self-consciousness, or inhibition—naturally. When we are physically free of accumulated bad habits and tension, we feel joy when we move—the joy that comes from physical freedom and good health. We become more confident, for when we control our physical response to a situation, our mental and emotional responses become more controlled also. William James, the father of psychology, found many years ago that action does not follow feeling, as is commonly supposed, but that in truth feeling follows action, and when we control the physical response to a situation, the emotional response follows accordingly.

For example: You are about to walk into a room full of strangers. As in any new situation, you are understandably slightly uncomfortable. However, because you have learned to appear self-confident through proper carriage and movements, you walk into the room with the appearance of confidence. People, impressed with your grace and bearing, respond to you in a positive way. You now feel, as well as look, confident. On the other hand, if you do not control your physical response to your initial anxiety, you will likely walk into the room with your head down, shoulders forward, and eyes averted. Your hands may be clenched, and your arms held close to your sides. People, aware that you are uncomfortable, will tend to leave you alone. You feel alien and unsure.

As important as posture is to beauty and health, it is absolutely indispensable to a youthful appearance. Yogis believe that you are only as young as your spine, and as long as the spine remains flexible, you remain youthful. Think for a moment of the flexibility of a child. The child gives no thought to aches or pains as he runs and jumps and shouts. His movements are quick and coordinated. Many of us lose that beautiful flexibility very early in life because of disuse. Inactivity breeds stiffness and hastens the aging process. It is necessary to stretch the spine every day to remain flexible. In this chapter are some exercises to help you achieve the suppleness that will put a spring in your step and a gleam in your eye.

A Personal Posture Analysis

In order to achieve beautiful posture, as with all the facets of our program, it is necessary to conduct an initial analysis of yourself. I suggest putting a full-length mirror against a wall or door at the end of a hall or long room. Walk toward your mirror image exactly as you would walk into a room, or down the street. Remember, it is important to be absolutely honest with yourself if you are to achieve results. Starting with the position of your head, you are going to analyze the different parts of your body that correspond to posture and write down the results on the chart provided.

POSTURE ANALYSIS CHART

From the Front:

Head _____

Neck _____

Shoulders _____

Chest _____

Diaphragm _____

From the Side:

Abdomen _____

Back (S-curve) _____

Knees _____

Arms _____

Hands _____

Feet _____

Stride _____

Note the position of the head: Is it straight, to one side, down, or up?

Closely observe the position of your neck as you walk toward the mirror. Does it come forward, lean to one side, or sit straight on your shoulders?

As you walk again toward the mirror, look at your shoulders. Are they back, down, or forward? Are they straight across, or is one higher than the other?

Focus your attention on your chest. Do your breasts droop or stick out, or do you pull your chest in? (Many large-breasted women unconsciously do this.)

Move your eyes down toward your diaphragm. Is there a considerable space between your waist and your chest?

Now turn sideways. You are going to walk back and forth in front of the mirror observing the rest of your body from the side.

Focus your attention on your abdomen. Be honest now: Does it protrude a little, or is it flat?

Observe the curve in your back between your waist and your buttocks. Is the curve obvious?

Now glance in the mirror at your legs as you stand or walk. Are your knees straight, or are they flexed slightly?

Look at the position of your arms. Are they held close to the body, or far from the body? Are the elbows stiff, or flexed?

Are the hands clenched, out at the sides, or relaxed?

Finally, walk forward toward your image again. Note the position of your feet. Do you toe in or out; do your feet crisscross over each other?

Is your stride long, short, or medium?

Record your findings on the posture chart. Each day check your image in the mirror as you consciously improve your posture. If your problem demands a couple of additional exercises, add them to your routine. Within a few short weeks you will be walking and standing with grace and confidence, and you will experience the joy and aliveness that come from knowing that your body is truly under your control.

The Head and Neck

The head should be held erect—the tip of the ear should be in line with the shoulder, the eyes should glance straight ahead. If your head is held too far up or down, practice walking toward yourself in the mirror until you become conscious of your correct position. An erect head and smiling face indicate a positive, confident personality.

The neck should be straight on the shoulders; it should not lean to the side, or come forward. Shoulders should not be "hunched" around the neck. I will never forget a beautiful blond model I knew who used to complain that her neck was too short. She had a traffic-stopping figure, which she exercised diligently, but her "short" neck was always a source of discomfort to her. At one point, she began to take dancing lessons from a very demanding instructor, who zeroed in on her problem. "You do not have a short neck," he barked. "Your problem is that you are holding all your tension in your neck and shoulders, and that you are bringing your shoulders up around your ears. Relax, stretch your head and neck upward, and your neck will grow!" The difference was amazing. My friend's neck "grew" within minutes, and she was never again self-conscious about it. If you feel that you hold a lot of tension in your neck, here is a good exercise that you can practice anytime.

The Neck and Head Roll

1 Sit up straight. Close your eyes and breathe deeply three times.

2 As you inhale for the fourth time, try to bring your right ear to your right shoulder. Do not raise your shoulder—keep both

125

shoulders straight. Continue to inhale as you roll your head back s-l-o-w-l-y, feeling the stretch in your neck. Bring your head completely around, and as you bring your left ear toward your left shoulder, begin to exhale. Continue to exhale as you return to your starting position.

3 Roll your head three times to the right, and then three times to the left. Be sure to exercise both sides.

4 After completing the exercise, breathe deeply again, keep your eyes closed for a moment, and observe the sensation of relaxation in your head and neck.

The Shoulders

Many of us, especially those in sedentary jobs, tend to hold tension in the shoulder area. This tension can be experienced as a painful knot between the shoulder blades or at the base of the neck. If you find your shoulders are stiff and sore after a few hours' work, or if they tense and raise, practice the Shoulder Roll and melt the tension away. The Yoga Mudra is also wonderful for the release of tension in this area and promotes good circulation too.

The Shoulder Roll

1 Sit up straight. Close your eyes and take three deep breaths. Consciously straighten your shoulders and bring them back and down.

2 Inhale as you bring your shoulders straight up toward your ears (as if you were shrugging them), and hold the position for a moment.

3 Bring your shoulders slowly back and down, in a rotating motion, until they are down as far as possible.

4 Begin to exhale as you bring your shoulders forward and up. Rotate the shoulders in this fashion three times backward, then three times forward.

Yoga Mudra

1 Sit on your heels on the floor. Put your hands on your knees, palms down. Take three deep breaths and relax.

2 On your fourth inhalation, begin to bring your hands around behind you, straighten your elbows, and clasp your fingers together.

3 Begin to exhale as you lean forward slowly from the waist, pulling the shoulders back and keeping the arms straight.

4 Rest your head on the floor in front of your knees, and try to point your clasped fingers and straight arms up toward the ceiling as far as possible. Keep your shoulders back, keep your arms straight, and relax the rest of your body, including your face. Breathe deeply three times, and feel the blood flow forward into your face. Remain in this position, breathing deeply, until the tips of your ears feel warm.

5 Inhale and slowly begin to sit up, keeping your shoulders back, elbows straight, and hands clasped.

6 Exhale, unclasp your fingers, and let your hands float forward until once again they rest on your knees.

127

The Diaphragm

Your diaphragm should be open also. Pull your chest up out of your waist—do not scrunch over—and enjoy the marvelous stretch in your spine. Especially if you are a desk sitter, remember to keep this area open, and consciously maintain a space between your lungs and your waist.

The Arms and Hands

You may not realize it, but your arms and hands are on display as you stand or walk. Often, people with otherwise faultless posture exhibit their tension in the arms and hands. The arms should be flexed slightly and swing loosely from the shoulders as you walk. The hands should be relaxed and in line with the rest of the arm. The following exercise will help you relax your arms:

The Hand Shake

1 Hold your arms on either side of you at waist level, elbows bent.

2 Shake your hands in all directions, trying to keep your elbows still. Pretend your hands are not even part of your body—shake the tension out of them until they are limp and loose and totally relaxed.

The Abdomen and Lower Back

Observe your abdomen closely from the side. Do you see a slight protrusion when you relax? Now shift your gaze to the area between your waist and lower back. Is the area relatively flat, or do you notice a rather pronounced S-curve? Many women have a definite problem with the lower back and with a slightly rounded tummy. Abdomen-strengthening exercises will help, but they may not rid you of this tummy, which is caused by lordosis, or lower back sway, and by incorrect spinal alignment. In many cases I recommend the services of a competent chiropractor. If the problem is not too pronounced, however, the following exercises will help to bring your spine back into proper alignment. The Rag Doll will not only help to straighten the spine, but also will release tension in the upper body and improve the complexion, due to increased circulation to the face.

The Rag Doll

1   Stand with your feet a foot apart, about a foot away from a wall. Rest your buttocks against the wall.

2   As you exhale, bend forward from the waist and let your head and arms dangle as though you were a rag doll. Feel the increased circulation in your neck and face. Remain in this position, breathing deeply, until the tips of your ears become warm.

3   Slowly begin to come up, touching one vertebra at a time to the wall. Pretend your spine is a string and every vertebra is a bead that you wish to align in a straight line. If your waist starts to come away from the wall, stop and press it again to the wall. Come up as far as you can without pulling your body away from the wall. Practice every day, until you can press your shoulders against the wall while your waist still touches the wall.

The Pelvic Tilt

1   Lie on the floor, with your knees bent and your feet flat on the floor, your arms resting at your sides. Press your lower back and waist firmly to the floor.

2   Very slowly straighten your right leg, keeping your lower back flat on the floor.

3   Straighten your left leg.

4   If possible, without arching the back, raise your right arm slowly, then your left arm. Hold this position for 60 seconds.

5   Slowly lower the right arm, then the left, and bring the legs back to the original position.

129

The Knee

The knee is an often neglected joint, and we rarely think of it as being of any use at all except to bend the leg. In fact, nothing could be further from the truth. The knee is the shock absorber of the whole body, and if it is locked when we stand or walk, we appear stiff and tense, not visually graceful. Believe it or not, fully 95 percent of my students walk with locked knees. The large muscles of the thighs and buttocks are meant to be used. When we actively use these muscles, and put our weight where it belongs, we also strengthen these muscles and keep these areas firm and unflabby. When, on the other hand, we lock our knees, all of the weight of the body is supported by the lower leg. This results in atrophy of the thigh and buttocks muscles from disuse, and in large calf muscles, swollen ankles and feet, and varicosities from overuse of the lower leg. When you flex your knees, you will find that your whole body becomes looser and more graceful. Your chest appears fuller, your waist smaller, the curve in your lower back is less noticeable, and your walk is much smoother, as well as more secure.

Try it now. Stand sideways in front of the mirror. Flex (do *not* bend) your knees and contract your abdomen slightly, and be aware of your more beautiful reflection. Some of my students have taken their waist measurements at this time and noticed a reduction of up to 1½ inches. Now try to walk, keeping the pelvis slightly forward, the knees and arms flexed, the head high, and the shoulders back and down. At first you will feel awkward. Do not give up! Remember, you are relearning how to walk, and just as a toddler is unsure at first, so will you be. But with daily practice in front of your mirror, you will soon find that good posture and a graceful gait happen automatically.

Here is an excellent exercise to increase the flexibility of your knees and strengthen the large muscles of the thighs and buttocks.

The Weight Roll

1   Bend your knees and put your hands on them. Keep your back straight, and make sure that your feet are pointing straight ahead. Put all your weight on your right knee.

2   Transfer the weight to both toes as you r-o-l-l forward. Keep your feet flexed; do not let the flat of your foot touch the floor.

3   Step forward with your left heel.

4   Transfer the weight again to both toes, alternating feet as you progress in a straight line. (Your balance may be off at first, and your line may not be so straight, but practice makes perfect.) Practice this exercise up and down a large room or hallway.

The Feet

Finally, observe your feet from the side as you walk. Is your gait right for your height? If you are petite, small steps are for you. If you are tall, a long stride is appropriate. Adjust your stride to your height, and practice, glancing sideways in the mirror, until you are comfortable and your new gait becomes second nature.

If your feet do not point straight ahead as you walk toward your reflection, practice walking with your feet in parallel lines, and practice the weight roll daily, until this becomes a habit. Crisscrossing or toeing out or in can result in weak and improperly developed leg muscles and a host of other problems, as I am sure any podiatrist or chiropractor would tell you.

Here are some additional hints to help you to attain a graceful walk:

■ Point with your knee, then follow with the foot. Think of a beautiful show horse walking gracefully, always leading with the knee.

■ Place your foot down flat when taking a step. Avoid hitting with the heel first, as this is a shock to the body, and appears visually as bouncing.

■ Keep your shoulders still but relaxed.

■ Tuck your derriere under.

■ Keep your head back, chin parallel to the floor.

■ Flex your knees slightly at all times. (Do not let them lock while you walk.) Remember, this will result in shapelier legs and buttocks as well as in a more beautiful posture and walk.

If your posture is less than perfect, you owe it to yourself to correct it. Not only will you exult in the feelings of health, joy, and self-confidence that result from true freedom of movement, but you will attract positive attention and remarks from others. You will appear far younger than your years as long as you remember that flexibility is the key.

Week Five

Relaxation and Stress Control

THIS is a good time to get a Polaroid picture taken of yourself. As all of us know, a picture is worth a thousand words, and at this point it's also tangible evidence of your amazing metamorphosis. Compare the "now" picture with one taken prior to the beginning of this program. View yourself with rightful pride as you note the many improvements in your figure, skin, and posture. Some of you may appear years younger already. Gloat a little—you deserve it!

This past week, you have been hard at work as you concentrated on making beautiful posture an important facet of your program. Unlike diet, exercise, and skin care, which can be practiced at specific times, the precepts of correct body alignment must be adhered to constantly. You have become very aware of others' posture, too—this is to be expected now as you continue to establish good habits and integrate them into your lifestyle. Perhaps, if you have lost or gained sufficient pounds, you are ready to adjust to our maintenance diet. Do not relax the diligence with which you perform your exercises—remember, you're still in basic training, and will be until your measurements reach the ideal you have set for yourself.

Your skin is positively glowing, and I'll bet that you've received compliments about it from more than one admirer. People are beginning to notice your improved carriage, too, and this makes you even more determined to continue your transformation. Best of all, you feel wonderful.

This week we're going to concentrate on a very important attribute of health and beauty—serenity, or relaxation. Through the posture exercises you have begun to release some of the long-held, unconscious tensions that marred the beauty of your carriage and movement. This week you're going to work at rooting out deeper tensions, thus freeing energy for use in a positive way. Work on your relaxation program every day this week, and notice and record in writing, at the end of each day, the effects of your new awareness and practice in this vital area.

The Problem of Stress

No discussion of your health would be complete without examining the problem of stress. Stress can manifest itself in a variety of physical and psychological ways, contributing to or causing such unwanted conditions as headaches, hives, hair loss, insomnia, digestive and eliminative disorders, ulcers, depression, and worse. Indeed, many medical practitioners believe that fully 80 percent of all disease, including cancer, is caused by stress. The incidence of stress-caused diseases is skyrocketing for working women in particular as they take on more and more of the pressures of a so-called "man's world." Heart attacks, high blood pressure, and strokes are only some of the serious problems that can result.

Doyennes of the beauty business tell us that relaxation is absolutely necessary for optimum good looks, too. When I began this program in 1974, relaxation was just a small part of it. I have now come to believe that another cornerstone in the building of beauty and health must of necessity be relaxation.

Not that stress can or should be banished totally from our

135

lives. A stressor is anything that threatens, prods, scares, worries, or thrills us, and sometimes it is exactly what we need to become motivated. Stress becomes a problem when we can no longer control our emotional or physical response to the stressor. Bottling it all up inside is not controlling stress, either.

We live in a complex, competitive, often negative society. From the time we are little children, many of us are conditioned to believe that we are not "good enough"—not pretty, smart, rich, etc., enough. Through the media, we are exposed to examples of wealth, beauty, intelligence, and morality at an early age, and, fearing that we can never meet those standards, we begin to feel inadequate, competitive, and jealous—naturally! Instead of accepting and liking ourselves for what we are, we either strive too hard to be perfect or give up entirely and take refuge in poor physical and emotional habits, which eventually begin to enslave us. Fear and insecurity about self-worth give rise to tremendous tension, and we become increasingly more pressured.

Feelings of inadequacy eventually are manifested in either a superiority or an inferiority complex, both of which prevent us from understanding and enjoying others.

Some of us take refuge in daydreaming, or in participating vicariously in the lives of television or movie characters (note the popularity of soap operas).

Some of us constantly feel sorry for ourselves because of what we don't have. The more we wish for tomorrow, the less satisfied we are with today.

In short, tension starts when we refuse to accept what really is. Only when we realize that most of us have too many wants and too many options—many of which, realistically, must remain unfulfilled—can we begin to concentrate on what is possible in our lives and act accordingly. We must also realize that, until now, most of us were unwilling victims of tension.

Now we have the power to change this condition once and for all.

A Personal Stress Check

This Stress Check was formulated by Lynn Kelleher, a certified Kripalu Yoga teacher who heads the relaxation section of our program. Lynn is one of the most relaxed women I have ever met, and one who truly enjoys life to the fullest. She credits this to her daily practice of relaxation techniques.

STRESS CHECK

Close your eyes for 60 seconds after reading this sentence and observe the state of your emotions and your mind. Now open your eyes.

■ What is the position of your feet? Are they held very close together? Are your toes curled and clenched? Assuming that you are seated, there is no need for the feet to be active or tense in any way. Relax your feet.

■ Check your legs. If they are crossed, uncross them. Both feet should be flat on the floor, a few inches apart. Relax your calves and thighs.

■ Now check the hips, buttocks, and pelvis. It is very common to hold tension in these areas—and very detrimental to both health and beauty. It is absolutely necessary, in order for your body's energy to move freely, to keep these parts of your body relaxed. Let go.

■ Focus your attention on your abdomen. Loosen your belt if it restricts you at all, and push your abdomen out for a moment. Feel these muscles pushing, and then consciously relax them. (If you find yourself wanting to "hold it in" because you would like a flatter tummy, don't. This will only create tension around your middle. Proper diet and exercise are the only way to tone and flatten the stomach.)

■ Check your chest and shoulders for stiffness. Let your chest expand and contract in conjunction with your breath. The shoulders should be down and relaxed. Are you holding them up toward your ears? Is one held higher than the other?

■ Concentrate on your arms and hands. Let them go totally limp. Are you beginning to be more relaxed?

■ What is the condition of your back? This is a frequent site of long-held tension. By simply focusing on the spinal column and the back muscles, you will begin to release and relax. Enjoy the feeling of relaxation.

■ Turn your attention to the neck and throat region. Many tension headaches can be relieved through gentle, slow neck rotations—first to the right, then to the left. Check your face. Relax your jaw, and part your lips slightly as you relax your mouth. Relax your forehead and the area around your temples. Feel that your face is expressionless.

■ Finally, close your eyes and rest them for a moment. Open them slowly.

When you focus your attention on the body, it begins to relax. A simple awareness exercise like this one, performed frequently, can do wonders to banish stress quickly and keep it from becoming chronic.

If the cause of your tension has been improper physical habits, you should be feeling more relaxed already as you follow this program. Improper diet, lack of exercise, and poor posture can wreak havoc on the body's ability to fight stress.

Barbara Thorpe, thirty-nine, of Loudonville, New York, came to this program when she was under a severe life stress. Her father had just passed away, and her husband's job necessitated a major move from the South to the North. She felt depressed and out of control. Barbara's mother had been a model; Barbara had always taken great pride in her appearance, and her figure had always been nothing short of eye-stopping. In her distressed state, however, Barbara began to eat too much of the wrong foods, stopped exercising, and developed a cellulite condition. Having been trained in behaviorial psychology, Barbara recognized the cause of her negative behavior and enrolled in our program, determined to nip the problem in the bud. She proved to be an outstanding student and in one week lost seven pounds and seven inches in all the right places. Her depression disappeared, and she lost her cravings for negative foods. Her skin glowed, her energy increased, and even an annoying sinus condition disappeared. Barbara has now followed the program for over a year and a half. She travels a lot (which is itself a stress), but sticks to her routine. Barbara's stress is well under control because she was wise enough to recognize the danger signals and then to take affirmative action.

For some of us, this is all that is needed. But for most of us, correcting diet, exercise, and posture alone is not enough to banish stress—we need to relearn how to let go. Confused by a society that constantly excites us, appeals to our senses, and demands perfection, we react instinctively with tension. But we can change inwardly, just as we have changed outwardly. And, as with all the other aspects of this program, we must first acknowledge our condition, and then realize that relaxation is our natural birthright and we must reclaim it.

Four Proven Methods of Stress Control

I suffered for years from tension. As a child, I constantly daydreamed about how perfect life would be when I became an adult. When I learned better, I foolishly transformed my dream to "when I become a model." I believed that when I attained a measure of beauty and grace, all my troubles would disappear and life would be a constant round of good times. This didn't happen either, and I often felt bitter, inadequate, and discontent—even amid the glamour and glitter of the modeling world. Then one day I began to work with a new photographer, who impressed me with his serenity and emotional stability. As it turned out, he had already suffered three nervous breakdowns from striving constantly for perfection. Although rich and famous, he had been tormented by his nerves, and seriously considered abandoning his profession. A relaxation technique called Transcendental Meditation, which he tried as a last resort, was responsible for changing his life.

I began to realize that stress was causing many of the problems in my life, and resolved to investigate TM, along with other relaxation techniques.

TRANSCENDENTAL MEDITATION

In 1971 I had an opportunity through my TV work to interview Maharishi Mahesh Yogi and attend a symposium given by him at the Massachusetts Institute of Technology. I was impressed, during the three days of the symposium, by the imposing array of medical personnel who attested to the health benefits of the TM program. Many lay people, too, reported that they were not only healthier but had experienced a newfound peace of mind shortly after they began to practice meditation regularly. My curiosity aroused, I decided to try the technique, and experienced an almost immediate improvement in my stress level. TM, I learned, must be practiced twice daily, for 20 minutes at a time, if it is to be truly effective. The TM technique consists of a mantra, a sound attuned to the needs of the recipient, which is "spoken" silently by the mind during the 20-minute period. When other thoughts begin to enter the mind, the student brings the attention back to the mantra, and after a short time the mantra begins to quiet the mind, which then enters a state of relaxation. This relaxation filters through to the physical body, and tension begins to dissipate. Following this period of stress release, the student rises and stretches, enjoying a renewed and strengthening energy.

Although the Maharishi has been the subject of much controversy, and although many other meditation techniques currently abound, I believe that the original TM program is one of the most valid relaxation tools available. There are TM Centers in most cities throughout the country, and by consulting your phone book or Information, you can locate one. If expense is a problem, there are many books available that describe the technique in detail. *The TM Book* by Denise Denniston and Peter McWilliams is excellent.

MASSAGE

A delightful and completely passive way to relax is to have a massage. Tension melts as the hands of an experienced masseuse or masseur soothe away worries, hurts, and anxieties. In addition to the delightful sensation of having your muscles stroked into serenity, massage is a wonderful aid in promoting good circulation, keeping the skin supple, and preventing or alleviating cellulite. During my pregnancy I made massage a weekly part of my health and beauty routine—consequently, I was not troubled by the varicosities, backaches, or stretch marks so common to women after giving birth.

Contrary to popular opinion, massage need not be expensive. Far more costly, in terms of both dollars and health, are tobacco, caffeine, and alcohol. If you are withdrawing from any of these, treat yourself to a month of massages—I'll bet it soon becomes a positive addiction!

YOGA

Even less expensive than massage is yoga. Quite simply, yoga *works*, but the key is a competent yoga teacher. In addition to relaxing the body and the mind, yoga helps to keep the body youthful through exercises that promote flexibility and suppleness. Yoga is good for the skin, too, because it improves circulation through inversion postures and breath control.

141

Later in this chapter you can practice some breathing exercises specially formulated for this program by Lynn Kelleher.

I have studied yoga for the past twelve years, and the most effective method I have found is the Kripalu Yoga Method, founded in this country by Yogi Amrit Desai. An instructor in this method must be certified, and there are Kripalu Yoga Centers springing up throughout the country. For more information about Kripalu Yoga, contact the Kripalu Yoga Retreat, Box 120, Summit Station, Pennsylvania 17979. Two excellent paperback books on yoga are *Yoga for Beauty and Health* by Eugene Rawls and Eve Diskin and *Yoga for Americans* by Indra Devi.

SELF-HYPNOSIS

A fourth technique that I consider to be most helpful in combating tension is self-hypnosis. Self-hypnosis is generally affordable and can be taught by a qualified hypnotherapist quickly and easily. At all times you are consciously aware of what is happening, although you are in a deep state of relaxation. While you are relaxing, you work with your subconscious mind to deprogram it of negative attitudes or habits. As with TM, in order to work properly self-hypnosis must be practiced daily. Twenty minutes is usually sufficient. Self-hypnosis can also be used to deprogram undesirable physical habits such as smoking and overeating. I have known individuals who, after one session with a hypnotist, dropped a cigarette habit that was a problem for many years.

The Importance of Sleep

On this health and beauty program, you should already be sleeping better. A nutritious diet high in Vitamins B and C (so easily lost through stress); the elimination of caffeine, alcohol, chocolate, sugar, and other stress-producing substances; and increased activity combine to make your rest fuller, deeper, and more refreshing. Sleep that is tranquil is one of the most beautifying and health-promoting aids available. When we sleep, the body rejuvenates itself—body functions slow down, and because the body is in a horizontal position the blood flows freely. The skin excretes toxic materials accumulated during the day, and the mind becomes quiet, calm, and rested.

After experiencing a good night's sleep, observe your face and skin the next day. You appear younger, lines and wrinkles are diminished, your color is deeper, and the whites of the eyes are clear and shiny. You feel energy coursing throughout the body and are relaxed and cheerful. No wonder we cherish a good night's sleep!

For those who suffer from insomnia, there are natural remedies available. Avoid over-the-counter sleep-inducing drugs, which can do far more harm than good and create a dependency. Also avoid alcohol as a sleeping aid, because research has shown that alcohol-induced sleep disrupts your natural sleep cycle and can leave you feeling nervous and exhausted in the morning. The good news for chronic (or occasional) sufferers from insomnia is that scientists have recently discovered that the amino acid L-tryptrophan induces drowsiness naturally and safely. This amino acid is used by the brain to produce serotonin. If you are not getting enough L-tryptophan with your food (turkey and dairy products are rich in it), or if your body is not absorbing it properly, the brain will not produce serotonin for your metabolic needs. This can result in such unpleasant symptoms as overaggression, depression, and insomnia. In 1978, in both the *Journal of the American Medical Association* and the *New England Journal of Medicine*, researchers reported on the negative effects of stress on the heart, and concluded that increasing the amount of serotonin in the body could significantly reduce the heart's vulnerability to stress-induced changes.

143

I personally know many physicians who suggest that their patients take L-tryptophan as a natural sleeping aid. The only caution of which I am aware is that if a Vitamin B_6 deficiency exists L-tryptophan can be harmful. (Women on the birth control pill should be aware that it decreases Vitamin B_6 levels in the body—another reason not to take the pill, if possible.)

Two physicians I interviewed, both authorities on mega-vitamin therapy, suggest 2 to 4 grams of L-tryptophan taken in conjunction with Vitamins B and B_6. The levels of B vitamins recommended for this program are high enough to be effective with L-tryptophan. L-tryptophan is most effective, in my experience, when taken half an hour before bedtime every night on a continuing basis.

TWO DRINKS TO HELP YOU SLEEP

If you suffer only from occasional, mild insomnia, here is a proven recipe that is effective in promoting healthy sleep and is inexpensive, highly nutritious, and delicious: Stir 1 tablespoon of blackstrap molasses into 1 cup of milk that has been heated to just short of boiling. The milk contains L-tryptophan and calcium, which is a natural tranquilizer; the molasses is rich in B vitamins.

Or try Sleepytime, an herbal tea by the Celestial Seasonings Company, which is a blend of chamomile and other sleep-inducing herbs. Sipped slowly before bedtime, it is a gentle sleeping aid.

Breathing for Relaxation

Right here and now, begin to experience the relaxation that occurs naturally when you learn to breathe correctly. Many people never think of breathing in conjunction with beauty and health, but without deep and full breath patterns we deprive ourselves of both physical and emotional health.

Try this experiment, designed by Lynn Kelleher to teach our students breathing awareness:

■ Imagine rush hour in Manhattan. Pretend you are walking on the street, you are late for an appointment, the streets are very noisy, it is a humid 90 degrees, and you are carrying a heavy suitcase. Breathe as if you were in this situation.

■ Now imagine that you are near the ocean, and there is a cool breeze blowing. It is early in the morning on the first day of your vacation. Breathe. Do you feel the difference?

For thousands of years yogis have recognized and studied the importance of breathing patterns to human health. Today, many of these same breathing exercises are given to business executives for stress management. Proper breathing is also being taught in conjunction with bioenergetics, psycho-therapy, and athletic training. I believe that in the future even more emphasis will be put on correct breathing, as we become more aware of just how effectively correct breath patterns banish stress.

BREATHING EXERCISES

Begin by breathing fully and deeply. Let your chest and abdomen rise and fall gently with each breath. Don't force or strain beyond your capacity. As you practice these exercises be sure to breathe in and out through your nose. Make sure that your posture is correct, so that you do not squash your diaphragm.

To Energize Yourself
Focus all your attention on your *inhalations* and visualize that you are drawing in the energy that brings you health and vitality, in the form of a white light. Imagine that you are near the ocean, or in a forest, and really feel yourself drawing in the

145

life-giving energy of the breath. Practice for 3 to 5 minutes, then let your breathing return to normal.

To Relax Yourself

Focus all your attention on the *exhalations*. Allow your breath to leave the lungs smoothly and slowly. Try to empty your lungs completely. As you exhale, visualize tensions being released along with the breath. Let go of all your anxieties with every exhalation. Practice this visualization for 3 to 5 minutes, and enjoy the peace that results.

Daily Exercises for Relaxation

During the next week, practice the exercises that follow twice daily. They take only a few minutes, and in addition to calming you, they will be beneficial to your skin and circulation and help to keep you youthful and flexible. It is necessary to practice them slowly and consciously, in a quiet room if at all possible. My students tell me that they are effective tension relievers after a hard day at work and promote a more restful sleep when used just before bedtime.

Alternate-Nostril Breathing

This exercise calms both body and mind. It also helps in overcoming headaches and insomnia and strengthens the nervous system when practiced regularly.

1 Sit in a cross-legged position. Place the tips of the index and middle fingers of your right hand against your forehead between your eyebrows; the right thumb rests lightly against the right nostril, the ring finger rests against the left nostril.

2 Press down on the right nostril with your thumb, and lift the finger from your left nostril and breathe in through it. Fill the lungs completely as you inhale for a slow count of 8.

3 Now press your ring finger on your left nostril, so that both nostrils are closed, and hold for a count of 4.

4 Raise your right thumb from your right nostril and exhale slowly for a count of 8. Repeat 7 times.

NOTE: When retaining the breath, it is helpful to lower your head so that your chin rests on the notch just above your breastbone. Raise your head slowly as you begin to exhale.

The Cobra

This exercise manipulates, stretches, and adjusts every vertebra of the spinal column. All muscles, tendons, and ligaments of the back are relaxed and relieved of tension and fatigue. When it is practiced regularly, the body is revitalized, posture improves, muscles of the back, chest, and bust are strengthened, and the buttocks are firmed.

1 Lie on your stomach, with your hands directly under your shoulder blades, heels together. Your head should rest with your forehead on the floor. Let the entire body go limp for a minute, as though you were a rag doll.

2 Very slowly, raise just your eyes upward as far as possible. When they can go no farther, raise your head, neck, and shoulders and then your trunk off the floor as far as possible. Do not use your arms and hands to help you—tense your buttocks muscles and use the muscles of your back to raise yourself. Take a full 20 seconds to achieve this posture.

3 Hold the posture for 10 seconds.

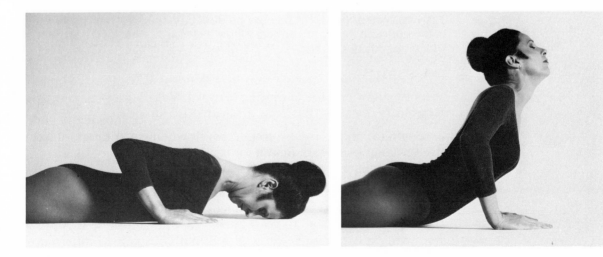

4 Slowly lower your trunk, one vertebra at a time, until your shoulders touch the floor.

5 Slowly lower your head, and finally your eyes. Rest your forehead on the floor and experience the release of tension. Repeat 3 times.

The Neck Stretch

This exercise relieves tension as it helps to relax the entire body. It also irons out tension lines in the face. It is very important during this exercise to move slowly and gently.

1 Lie in the same position as for the Cobra. Prop yourself up on your elbows and rest your chin in your cupped hands.

2 Turn your head to the left, so that your chin rests in your left hand and the back of your head is in your right hand.

3 Turn your head as far to the left as it will go without undue strain, and with only the most gentle help from your hands. Hold this stretch for 5 seconds.

4 Turn your head very slowly to the right, until your chin is tucked in your right hand and the back of your head rests on the left hand. Repeat this complete exercise 3 times; work up to holding the position for 20 seconds on each side.

The Forehead-to-Heels Stretch

The Cobra stretches the spine in one direction; this exercise stretches it in the opposite direction. Always follow a forward or backward stretch with an opposite stretch.

1 Sit on the floor. Stretch your legs out directly in front of you, heels together and toes pointing forward. Make sure your posture is tall from the waist up. Your arms are at your sides.

2 Begin to inhale, and as you do so, slowly raise your arms and stretch them overhead. Reach for the ceiling as you hold your breath momentarily.

3 Begin to exhale as you lower your arms and trunk toward your outstretched legs, keeping your knees straight and feet together. Try to touch your head to your knees—if you cannot do this at first, with daily practice you will find that your spine limbers up quickly.

4   Rest your elbows on the floor next to your knees and relax. Breathe deeply 3 times in this position.

5   Slowly, inhale as you begin to raise your head and upper body. Continue upward until you reach your original position. Repeat 3 times.

Relax on Your Slant Board

I would like to emphasize once again the importance of the slant board as an invaluable aid to relaxation, beauty, youthfulness, and health. I seriously hope that you will make the slant board part of the rest of your life. Remember that when the feet are higher than the head, pressure on the veins and arteries of the legs is lessened, which reduces the possibility of varicose veins, swollen ankles, and cellulite. In addition, increased circulation promotes relaxation, and ultimately better circulation, which brightens the complexion. The hair and scalp benefit from the increased circulation too, and even the brain becomes more alert. In this position, the back flattens and the spine straightens itself. Abdominal muscles, which have a tendency to sag, experience a natural lift, and all body muscles enjoy a temporary release of physical tension. To further your relaxed state while you are on the slant board, listen to some music specifically designed for relaxation.

The Rejuvenating Effects of Water

Ever since I enjoyed my first mineral bath at the Saratoga Spa in Saratoga Springs, New York, fifteen years ago, I have been convinced of the curative power of water for nervous disorders. I didn't know then that minerals are absorbed through the skin, and that in many controlled experiments both in the U.S. and in Europe mineral waters have been proven to have a beneficial effect on the connective tissues of the body, as well

149

as positive psychological effects. For many hundreds of years, water has been used as a healing agent for people suffering from many different ailments, ranging from premature aging to stress-induced disorders. All I knew, after my first mineral bath, was that I felt wonderfully calm and relaxed. A glance in the mirror showed that I looked more rested, too.

Although I strongly recommend the real honest-to-goodness spa waters as both stress-reducing and rejuvenating, I am well aware that not all of you are lucky enough to live near a health spa. I do think, though, that we can use our own bathrooms as inexpensive but effective "spas" to help us relax. Try the following treatments:

If you have had a hard day, slip into a soft robe. Lower the lights in your bathroom, and begin to fill the tub with warm water. (The temperature should be about 2 degrees higher than your body temperature. Invest in a bath thermometer.) Put some classical music on the stereo. Light a scented candle and put it somewhere safe where you can enjoy its glow. Blend ½ cup sweet almond oil with 1 quart whole milk and add it to your bath. Relax in the tub for at least 15 minutes. Concentrate on the music, and if disturbing thoughts enter your mind, gently turn them off by focusing your attention on the sounds of the great composers. This is a gentle discipline that works. If you are so inclined, sip a cup of hot chamomile tea or, if weight is not a problem, a cup of warm milk and molasses. Following this period of relaxation, gently soap and loofah your body. Pat yourself dry with a fluffy towel, smooth scented cream on your body, and either take a 15-minute nap or rest, or enjoy a good night's sleep.

One of my students who is a traveling executive packs a mini-candle, nonfat dry milk powder, a plastic container of sweet almond oil, scented soap leaves, and a loofah along with her makeup. These items take up very little space, weigh practically nothing, and, according to her, have "saved my sanity" at the end of more than one highly pressured day.

If you'd like to know more about the health and beauty benefits of baths and spas I recommend reading *Secrets from the Super Spas* by Emily Wilkins, *Health Secrets from Europe* by Paavo O. Airola, and *Jeanne Rose's Herbal Body Book*.

Another way to strengthen the nervous system naturally is to use alternating warm and cold showers. Yes, I know it sounds masochistic, but it works, especially first thing in the morning. For many years Europeans have used cold water as a health restorer, strengthening agent, and skin rejuvenator. They know that cold water stimulates the glandular system, speeds up metabolism, builds resistance to infection and stress, and helps keep them looking young and wrinkle-free.

I admit that it does take getting used to. After your morning exercise session, shower with warm water and your loofah, then finish with a cool-to-cold shower of at least 60 seconds. Once this routine becomes a habit, it actually begins to feel good. You will love the way your skin glows, and you will feel stronger and more energetic all day. (Caution: If you have any serious physical ailments, consult your physician before commencing this treatment.)

Relaxation as a Way of Life

As we come to the end of this chapter on relaxation, I would like to tell you the story of one of the most relaxed, yet most active, women I know. Her name is Grace Jorgensen Westney, and she is the doctor who inspired me, so long ago, to begin my study of nutrition and its effects on health and beauty. This busy woman, who is the administrator of Bellevue Maternity Hospital in Schnectady, New York, also maintains a large private practice in obstetrics and gynecology, serves on the boards of directors of a woman's college and a bank, is active in community affairs, and is a devoted wife and mother. Grace strongly believes that good nutrition and exercise are necessary basics for health and vitality. She jumps rope every morning, sometimes to music, often outdoors if the weather permits. During the day she makes sure to eat slowly and at regular times, and includes low-fat cheeses, nuts, and fruits in her diet for sustained energy. She strictly avoids drugs and cigarettes. She makes sure that her environment is pleasant, with a focus on beauty. Her hospital is a testimonial to this belief—beautiful plants abound and the rooms are furnished tastefully, with carpets on the floors and wallpaper on the walls. The food is nutritious and delicious—for example, on Fridays patients are treated to a special luncheon of lobster tails, and on Wednesday evenings wine is provided with supper. Grace approaches her work with a positive attitude—she loves her practice and considers running the hospital a challenge. She believes in trying her best, but does not berate herself unnecessarily when disappointments and failure occasionally occur. She begins each day by making a realistic list of things that can be accomplished. She tries to do the least interesting things first, as they generally take more energy. Grace strongly believes in the strength of a close family. Her husband and three children are very dear to her, and she elects to spend her free time with them pursuing healthful and relaxing hobbies such as gardening, music, cooking, and hiking. She makes a point of traveling to the country once a week, on her day off, to refresh and renew her spirits.

During a busy day at the hospital, she takes at least one 10-minute relaxation break to recharge her energy. At the end of her long day, she relaxes each evening with her husband—their dinner together is a reward for a job well done.

Grace Jorgensen is one of the few women I have ever met whose face shows no evidence of stress lines. It is just about impossible to guess her age from her appearance—her figure is beautiful, her posture is perfect, her skin glows with good health. Her enjoyment of life is evident to all who meet her.

I urge you to begin today to enjoy *your* life to the fullest. There is no better time. You are taking great care of yourself with your program. Smooth out the furrows in your forehead, relax your shoulders, put on a happy face, and put a spring in your step.

Week Six

A Lifetime Maintenance Regime

O VER the past six weeks you have undergone a metamorphosis. You have conscientiously been following the diet most suited to your needs since Week One. As
a result, your energy level is now higher than you ever
dreamed possible, your skin is glowing and translucent, and
shadows and under-eye circles are no longer visible. Your hair
and nails are stronger and longer, and your eyes are clear and
shining. You possess a beauty that you could never have found
in a jar or bottle. You truly are what you eat!

Since Week Two, the Body Sculpting regime has become a
daily part of your life. You have scheduled it into your day at a
time convenient for you, and you accept no excuse to deviate
from your schedule. You know that it is "magic" for your figure, and that now you can have the youthful-looking body of
your dreams. Saddlebag thighs no longer trouble you, your
abdomen is firmer and flatter, your waist more defined, your
breasts are becoming firmer, and your upper arms and inner
thighs more taut. Your high-repetition exercise regimen has
worked quickly and effectively, and you are fast becoming
proud of your body.

The simple routine of care for your skin that you began in
Week Three has simplified your life in terms of both time and
expense. No longer do you go from one product to another,
wondering if this is the magic cream or lotion that will transform you. You know that beauty foods like yogurt, water, and

yeast, used both from within and from without, do far more to produce a flawless complexion than a combination of chemicals enclosed in a seductive package. Your simple skin care program has become an easy and enjoyable part of your health and beauty routines.

For two weeks you have been aware of your posture and have been working to correct any imperfections in it. You now know that body alignment affects your health and beauty in a very definite way, and you are feeling the heightened confidence and pride that come from moving with control and grace.

Since last week you have been very aware of the necessity of daily relaxation and have been working to achieve it. You have been organizing your day a little better, thinking more positively, enjoying the present, and releasing tension through breath control and exercise. You are sleeping better, looking prettier, and enjoying life more. If cellulite has been a problem for you in the past, you know now that the combination of diet, exercise, skin care, posture, and relaxation can rid you of its embarrassing unsightliness once and for all. There is no need to waste money on gimmicks and gadgets.

I know for certain that if you have been faithfully following this program for the past five weeks, you are now experiencing a new vibrancy and vitality, and it is my purpose in this final chapter to teach you to retain both for the rest of your life. Perhaps the most difficult part of any program is maintenance. We must always remember that in order to retain value of any sort, constant care is necessary. Some people, once their goal is achieved, relax their efforts and backslide slowly, sometimes almost imperceptibly, into their former negative habits. Others, in a burst of self-pity, undo all the good they have done in a giant self-destructive binge and wind up feeling worse than when they started. Everyone backslides occasionally, but in my experience the results of deviating from this program (lack of energy, under-eye circles, cellulite, etc.) become apparent so quickly that the student immediately resumes her beauty and health routine. The majority of my former students touch base with me from time to time, and report that maintenance becomes a way of life after a short time, and actually becomes a real pleasure.

As I write this, I am motivated by this afternoon's appointment with one of my most recent students, Lois Staffin, a thirty-nine-year-old businesswoman who came to me just three months ago lacking energy, with quite a bit of cellulite on her legs, and with headaches and sinus problems. But Lois's main problem was a figure way out of proportion, which was making her miserable. Her measurements were 34-27½-39½, with 23½-inch thighs. Now her measurements are a perfect 34-23-33½, with 19½-inch thighs. Her cellulite is completely gone, and her figure could rival that of any girl of twenty. Her headaches and sinus problems have improved too, and she tells me that now she rises happily at 6:00 A.M., whereas before she dragged out of bed at 8:30 A.M. Her boyfriend is so impressed by her transformation that he is considering a major diet and exercise overhaul for himself! Through the dedicated performance of this program, Lois has managed to literally turn back the clock, and with continued vigilance she will look beautiful and vital for many years to come. Lois tells me she knows it will not always be easy to stick to her maintenance regime, but she has learned, as I hope you have, to love herself enough to be motivated to look and feel her best forever.

Let us consider the last five weeks as basic training. If you have reached your ideal weight, or have lost your cellulite, adjust your routine to the maintenance diet. If you have not yet reached your goal, continue your diet plan until you are perfectly happy with your weight. Do not resort to crash or fad measures. Continue your beautiful progress, and you will soon reach not only your ideal weight but your optimum beauty and health potential.

When you do begin your maintenance diet, for the first two weeks weigh yourself daily and record any fluctuations in weight. If there is a rise or drop in weight that lasts for three days, subtract or add foods totaling 200 calories each day. Then monitor your weight carefully for three more days. Make another 200-calorie adjustment, if necessary. If your weight increases or decreases more than 2 pounds from your ideal, resume your losing or gaining diet until you are back to your correct weight. With awareness, you will never again be embarrassed by a lack, or excess, of flesh. Always stay within 2 pounds of your ideal.

Once a week, treat yourself to a very special meal—I insist! Whether you cook at home or frequent the best restaurant you can find, make this meal a very special occasion. Plan on a leisurely lunch or dinner, and don't allow anything to interfere with your enjoyment. If you're tempted to include a food I listed as incompatible with health and beauty, go ahead! Try to share this special time with someone you genuinely love, and dress up for this occasion, too. Make sure that your surroundings are beautiful and peaceful. Tension at mealtime can be destructive to your health and interfere with your digestive process. I want this special meal to become a once-a-week holiday that will bring you hours of joy, and consequently, many happy memories. Just for curiosity's sake, keep a little diary of the foods you enjoy at these meals. As the weeks go by, your favorite foods will change noticeably, and you will soon see, with satisfaction, that negative eating preferences no longer dominate you. Note, too, how you feel after eating this meal.

On the day following your special meal, enjoy a juice or fruit fast. Especially if you have really binged at your festive meal, it is wise to detoxify your system and break the circle of any cravings you may have rekindled. It is very easy, during a busy Monday for example, to take only juice or a "mono meal" of one type of fruit. If your weight is ideal or if you are underweight, you may drink as much fruit or vegetable juice as you wish; if you have gained a few pounds, dilute the juice by half with spring water and take only at mealtime. Remember to include eight glasses of pure spring water on your modified fast. If you want to take your mono meal in the form of a whole fruit or vegetable, pick one that is low in calories (unless you are underweight, in which case choose bananas or grapes). Eat as much as you wish at mealtime. Drink spring water in between. This will become a delightfully easy habit after a few weeks. In your diary note your energy level and appearance the day following this beauty fast. From personal experience, I can tell you that I have come to love my own mini-fast. The rise in energy that I experience the next day, the clarity of my skin and eyes, and the loss of any excess body fluid are worthwhile rewards for this small discipline.

Europeans, who long have believed in preventive rather than curative health measures, generally incorporate a more extended, complete fast in their lives once or twice a year to give their bodies a housecleaning. There are many fasting resorts and spas throughout Europe, where whole families participate in the detoxifying process, enjoy the waters, and just relax. A week's fast is not difficult, if you have been following a program such as this, because large numbers of toxins have already been released. (I do not advocate a complete fast for anyone who has been abusing herself with junk foods, stimulants, or the like, for the side effects can be severe.) After two or three days, there is no desire for food. As toxins are being eliminated, the fasting person may notice increased perspiration, a slight headache, a metallic taste in the mouth, or slight dizziness as a result, but nothing more serious. Soon the faster enjoys a heightened sense of well-being that is hard to describe. The energy level rises, the skin absolutely radiates good health, and minor ailments, lumps, bumps, and bulges "miraculously" disappear. I asked Dr. Alan Immerman, consultant to the Pawling Health Manor at Hyde Park, New York, some of the more specific health benefits of fasting. He told me that they include safe and rapid weight loss, lowering of high blood pressure, breakdown of fat deposits in the blood vessels, lower blood sugar levels in diabetics, and relief of pain from arthritis. During a recent fast at the Manor, I met many people who absolutely swore by the fast as a method of alleviating health problems, from allergies to cancer. Sometime in the future, after you have become accustomed to partial fasts, you may wish to undertake a supervised fast for a week.

At least once a week, aside from your fruit-fast day, try to eliminate meat from your diet entirely, and note the results. I have already given you a recipe for vegetable quiche, and there are many excellent vegetarian cookbooks available. Through my own research and discussions with different health and beauty experts, I have come to believe that eliminating animal products from our diet as much as possible will keep us youthful for a very long time. An example of a person living this kind of vegetarian life is Joy Gross, director of the Pawling Health Manor and author of *The 30-Day Way to a Born-Again Body.* She is also the mother of five children and grandmother of one. Joy is fifty-four years old and appears to be no older than thirty-five, at most. She attributes her amazing beauty and vitality to her simple health and beauty routine, which revolves around her practice of vegetarianism. Joy dramatically improved her beauty and health at the age of fifteen, when she rid herself of a severe skin condition by turning to fasting and to a meatless diet. Since then, she has been a dedicated advocate of healthy living, and every day she guards her beauty and health by eating lots of green salads, fruits, and vegetables. She exercises daily, enjoys healthful hobbies, and uses makeup based upon natural products. Joy has learned that simplicity in living is the secret to youthfulness, and I pass her example on to you in the hope that you too may consider vegetarianism as an option for your life, either now or in the future. In any event, one day of meatless eating, plus your fasting day of beauty, will produce dramatic results.

Your exercise routine has been strenous for the last few weeks, but it has been well worth it as you realize . . . yes . . . you *can* have a dramatically improved figure! It will be necessary to maintain your measurements through attention to daily exercise, but the good news is that you no longer have to spend a half hour or more on your Body Sculpting routine. Twenty minutes daily is usually sufficient to maintain your shape. Remember, though, that for optimum endurance and energy I do suggest a strenuous workout (be it a sport or an aerobic routine) twice weekly in addition to the program. Divide your exercises into two categories—those for the bust, waist, and abdomen and those for the hips, buttocks, and legs. Continue half the number of repetitions (with the exception of the bust exercise) every other day. If one of your measurements decreases from your ideal, cut the exercise for that portion of your body in half once again. If your bust increases by an inch too much, eliminate the Flys from your routine for two weeks, and then measure. Generally speaking, once you reach your ideal it is necessary to concentrate heavily only on those areas that have a hereditary tendency toward under- or overdevelopment. For example: You had heavy thighs. You have been practicing 200 Thigh Slaps daily, and the thighs have reached ideal proportions. To maintain their svelte shape, do 100 Thigh Slaps every other day. If your thigh measurement should decrease further, reduce your Thigh Slaps to 50 repetitions. You will always have a tendency toward heavy thighs, but you need never again suffer from them.

The main principle to remember is *exercise faithfully every day.* I have found that these exercises, performed every morning, afford me an energy that I have come to rely on for the rest of the day. The few minutes spent in vigorous activity is good insurance against cellulite, figure problems, poor circulation, energy lag, and stiffness. Another principle that must be adhered to, strictly, is *weigh and measure once a week, every single week.*

Keep a close check on your skin, and adjust your skin care system accordingly. Many people notice an increase in the flow of oil as summer nears, and normal skin may be categorized as oily at this time. During the summer, then, switch to the recommended treatment for oily skin. Conversely, in cold weather the skin may begin to dry out, and appropriate adjustments in the routine should be made. Be scrupulous in your once-a-week skin care routine, and remember not to succumb to exotic, temptingly packaged new products that might hurt rather than help you. Skin that is treated naturally, gently, and lovingly will respond far better than skin that is slathered with expensive creams. The simple routine you have been following will save you time and money. It will also eliminate confusion about what to buy, and leave you more time for the really important priorities in your life.

Every day, maintain an awareness of your posture and practice correct body alignment. The hardest part is over—getting started! Within a few weeks, or at most two months, you will have developed new posture habits that will benefit your beauty and health for a lifetime. Models learn early the importance of good posture, and consciously strive to maintain a lifetime awareness of it. Claudie McGuire, a former Paris couture model who was associated with Nina Blanchard in this country, is a dear friend of mine. At forty-eight she still has the figure of a young girl, and all heads turn when this gorgeous woman walks into a room or down the street. Claudie attributes her beauty and lovely figure to a simple program of diet, exercise, and skin care, but most of all to correct body alignment. She maintains that the good posture habits she learned as a young model of sixteen are what has kept her body firm and supple ever since.

Remember that stress is an enemy of beauty and health, not to mention the fact that it takes the joy out of life. Practice your relaxation techniques and pay attention to this aspect of health and beauty just as you do to the more immediately visible ones. The physical, emotional, and mental benefits will be enormous. Enjoy stretching and stress-releasing exercises during your work breaks, and take a longer break before dinner, if possible. Give yourself the Stress Check every day, and, if necessary, incorporate meditation, massage, or another relaxation therapy into your life.

A Daily Routine

Making a schedule and sticking to it as much as possible is helpful in maintaining a beauty and health routine. Post your schedule on your closet door, or some other place that you see every day. Although no one can adhere rigidly to such a routine, it will act as a constant reminder that you are an important person and deserve to be good to yourself. Here is an example of a daily schedule, which could fit in with a working woman's routine:

7:00 A.M.	Wake-up and stretching exercises
7:05 A.M.	Body Sculpting exercises
7:25 A.M.	Breakfast. If time allows, enjoy it leisurely. If not, make an instant meal and drink it slowly.
7:35 A.M.	Wash, brush teeth, get ready for work
8:15 A.M.	Leave for work
8:30 A.M.–10:30 A.M.	Work
10:30 A.M.	Energy break (yeast and juice), a few unwinding exercises
10:45–Noon	Work
Noon	Enjoy lunch thoroughly. Do not rush. If time permits, enjoy a short walk in the fresh air. Do

not skip lunch—if you are overloaded with work and have no time for lunch, take a few minutes to slowly sip an instant meal.

12:30 P.M.–2:30 P.M.	Work
2:30 P.M.	Energy break (yeast and juice), a few minutes of unwinding exercises
2:45–5:00 P.M.	Work
5:30 P.M.	Home! Take a few minutes for yourself on the slant board, or practice another relaxation routine. Breathe deeply to release tension.
6:00 P.M.	Enjoy preparing and eating dinner, leisurely. Spend the evening doing something that brings you pleasure. Forget the tensions of the day and try to switch gears completely. Life is too short to be taken so seriously.

Before bedtime, remember your skin care system (including nonfat dry milk powder in your bath and body lotion). Exfoliate your body and face and wash and condition your hair.

Sip a cup of chamomile tea or a cup of hot milk just before sleep, if you wish . . . and pleasant dreams!

A Weekly Maintenance Routine

Spend one evening a week on yourself. Let nothing interfere with this ritual. Your family and friends will be happier to be with you because you will be happier with yourself, knowing you look and feel your best. The time and attention you spend on your wardrobe, skin, hair, and nails will make you a more attractive and confident person:

- Steam your face.
- Give yourself a mask.
- Manicure your nails.
- Deep-condition your hair.
- Repair clothing worn during the week. Iron and coordinate your wardrobe for the following week.

165

■ Experiment with new makeup colors and techniques—stay abreast of fashion. Becoming dated is the quickest way to appear old.

If you think that one evening per week is too much time to take from your busy schedule, try adding up the hours you have spent in the past trying to make last-minute, hurry-up preparations, and in getting nervous and upset. This one evening, well organized, will save you many hours in the long run. Make it an indispensable part of your week.

When You Travel

It is no longer considered unusual for businesswomen to spend time on the road. This program can be easily adapted to a traveling woman's schedule, and there is no excuse for backsliding when you follow these simple suggestions:

■ Measure out the vitamin supplements you will need and pack them in a small airtight box that you can keep in your purse. Many health food stores carry containers for just this purpose.

■ Measure out the amount of brewer's yeast you will need and seal it in a plastic bag with a measuring spoon.

■ Tuck a few small cans of unsweetened grapefruit juice or low-sodium V-8 into your suitcase. They are small and light—bring 2 per day for your beauty break.

■ If you enjoy an instant meal in the morning, bring a small plastic shaker jar (Tupperware has a terrific one for about three dollars). Pack nonfat dry milk powder as you do your yeast. Order orange or apple juice and a raw egg from room service. Combine with the milk powder, shake very well, and you're all set.

■ Forbid yourself any alcoholic beverages during the week, and adhere to this rule rigidly.

■ Upon arriving in a new town, call the local health food store for suggestions on where to find wholesome, attractively served meals. If you do not have time for this, choose only fresh beauty- and health-making foods from whatever restaurant you visit, and be an active consumer—be specific as to your preferences.

■ Plan to practice your exercise program first thing every morning, and allow time for it. Let nothing interfere.

■ Bring small plastic containers of nonfat dry milk, Vaseline, Aapri Scrub, and a mask (Queen Helene Mint Julep Masque, inexpensive and available in health food stores, is a good one) as well as nonallergenic freshener and moisturizer. The Vaseline and nonfat dry milk can be used to soften and moisturize your body as well as your face. Don't forget a travel-sized loofah. A small, inexpensive makeup kit will facilitate transporting your skin care products.

■ Practice your relaxation break *without* fail as you switch gears from the day to the evening. Travel is itself a stress on the body.

■ Do not neglect your once-a-week health and beauty routine. Schedule it just before your trip and you will enjoy the peace of mind that comes from being totally well groomed and well organized.

Become a Restaurant Critic

One of life's biggest pleasures is dining out in a pleasant atmosphere. There is nothing to do except relax and enjoy someone else's preparation of a taste-tempting meal. The secret to guiltless restaurant eating is being discriminating in your choice of eating establishments. Before you make reservations, ask if your food can be cooked to order, if whole-grain breads and rolls are served, and if the entrees and vegetables are fresh. If something does not please you, or if it has not been cooked as you indicated, do not hesitate to send it back. Learn to be an active consumer—it's your money and your right. I have found that most restaurants appreciate such honesty, and would rather correct their mistakes than have an unhappy customer leave, never to return. Remember, the function of restaurants is to serve you—and you're paying them well for gracious service.

Before you order, observe the food being served around you. Is that a heavy sauce on the fish? Are those carrots swimming in butter? You'll have a better idea of what to order if you keep your eyes and ears open. Ask for dressings and sauces on the side—that way, you'll be able to control the amount and consume less calories. And never be afraid to inquire about the ingredients. If they do not meet your requirements, pass them up and ask instead for oil and lemon or for the pepper mill.

In place of heavy desserts, most restaurants offer fresh fruits in season, or a combination of fruit and cheese. Except on your once-a-week holiday, or an occasional birthday, avoid rich desserts. They are heavy and bloating, and make weight control a real problem for all but the underweight. Even fruit and cheese can make you awfully fat in a very short time, but moderate amounts will give you more satisfaction and high energy in the long run than heavy cakes or pies. Just by consuming them, you are reaping benefits for your skin and hair and assuring yourself of a high energy level. Make every mouthful count toward your ultimate good.

What About Family and Friends?

This entire program is designed to become second nature to you, and your family and friends will soon become aware of your new, positive attitude toward yourself. You will become a shining example of health and beauty, and don't be surprised if they ask you to share your secrets with them. Be generous! Tell them about your program when they ask, but never preach at them.

It can be fun to teach your family about nutrition, exercise, skin care, posture, and relaxation. Teenage children, in particular, respond well to this program. At a time in their lives when they are self-conscious and indecisive, learning to look and feel their best can instill in them a sense of confidence and purpose that will be a lifelong benefit. Include your man in your program, too, if he is so inclined. Men suffer even more than women from the effects of poor nutrition and bad health habits. Let your man know that his attractiveness is important to you, as yours is to him. Chances are that his vanity will rise to the occasion and he will join you in your pursuit of good looks and good health. My husband, who is also my business partner, practices this program along with me. He is forty-three years old, is in terrific shape (most people think he is in his late twenties or early thirties), and has none of the physical problems of a middle-aged man (with the exception of a little arthritis, which bothers him only when he deviates from his healthy diet). We enjoy eating for health and exercising together. We practice yoga and take a class together once a week. Because health is another interest we have in common, our relationship is more rewarding.

Do not try to change your friends' ways by preaching to them. Your newfound beauty and energy will be enough to pique their curiosity. If they ask for advice, offer helpful suggestions, but never in a pompous or patronizing manner. Do not give in to the negative influences of your friends, either. Reject the offer of a sugar doughnut or a drink with a gentle "No, thank you" and a smile. Offer no explanations or excuses; you will be admired all the more for your goodwill. When you are at a friend's home for dinner and she prepares a meal that conflicts with your new eating plan, be tactful but stick to your diet. I have found that the easiest way around this dilemma is to eat a large portion of any allowable food—for example, vegetable salad and chicken—and let your hostess know how much you enjoy it. Simply pass up the starchy white pasta, white rolls, or oversauced vegetables with "I really prefer the chicken, thank you." She'll be flattered that you are enjoying her salad and chicken so much and will not be offended by your refusal of the less desirable food, as long as you refuse in a gracious and unobtrusive manner. I have never visited a friend's home where there was absolutely nothing that I could eat. Where there's a will, there's a way!

When you entertain at home, you can show your guests that healthy eating can be fun and delicious. One of the most elegant, and healthiest, parties I've ever attended was a buffet dinner given a few years ago by Eleanor Lambert, creator of the Coty Award, during her Fashion Week for the Press. Her dining room was beautifully appointed with candles, flowers, and gleaming silver. On the table was an enormous platter of raw vegetables, a tempting chicken pot pie, spinach fettuccine, a poached whole fish, a huge salad with a variety of healthful dressings, and rice crackers instead of bread. A variety of hot beverages, lush berries and fruits, and gourmet cheeses graced the sideboard. The guests thoroughly enjoyed the party, and as I savored my meal I heard nothing but glowing praise for the selection, tastes, and textures of the food, as well as the style with which it was presented. When I asked Miss Lambert some of her secrets for successful entertaining, she stressed the use of fresh herbs for seasonings, insistence on quality rather than quantity, use of fresh flowers, fruits, and vegetables for garnishes and decoration, and simplicity in both food combinations and preparations.

A Final Word

Entertaining, traveling, working, playing . . . each day we have an opportunity to grow, to improve. This program is my gift to you. With it, may you realize the health, beauty, vitality, and self-confidence that come when you truly learn to *care* for yourself.

Appendix:
Charting
Your
Progress

	PRESENT	WEEK ONE	WEEK TWO	WEEK THREE
Weight				
Bust				
Waist				
Abdomen or upper hip				
Lower hip				
Thigh				
Knee				
Calf				
Ankle				

Index